Warfare and Fortifications in the Borders

by John Dent & Rory McDonald

Scottish Borders Council
Department of Planning and Development

Scottish
Borders
C O U N C I L

A British Library Cataloguing-in-Publication Data record for this book is available from the British Library

ISBN: 0 9530438 2 7

Designed by the Graphics Section
Scottish Borders Council
Printed and bound by Buccleuch Printers Ltd., Carnarvon Street, Hawick TD9 7EB

First Published 2000. Reprinted 2004.
Department of Planning & Development, Scottish Borders Council

Foreword

The Anglo-Scottish frontier is arguably the most beautiful, and certainly the most bloodstained, region of Britain, perhaps of all Europe. For centuries it was the scene of internecine warfare between England and Scotland, in which great battles were fought, vast areas scorched into wilderness, towns and villages and magnificent abbeys were destroyed, and countless Borderers on both sides were killed. Even in times of official peace between the realms, the violence continued, for the people of the six Border marches, hardened by generations of slaughter, plunder, and guerrilla existence, carried on the tradition of raid and feud learned in war time. The great "riding families", Scottish and English, and the outlaw bands and "broken men", preyed continually along the line, setting their respective rulers at defiance, creating what amounted to a lawless no-man's-land between the two countries, until the accession of King James VI and I brought about the Union of the Crowns, and in a few short years the Border Reivers were swept from the frontier.

No part of that frontier had suffered more than the Scottish Middle and East marches, an area now known simply as "the Borders", although it makes up only a quarter of the Borderland proper. Here the English armies wrought ruin on a huge scale, culminating in the "Rough Wooing" of King Henry VIII's time, that futile attempt to bring about a marriage between the heirs to the two thrones.

The beautiful ruins of the Scottish abbeys are the heritage of those terrible years; equally evocative are the castles and strongholds which still endure all across the Border country, especially those sturdy little towers, known as peels or peles, in which the reiving families defied besiegers and sallied out on their raids.

The purpose of this book is to explain the historical background to the Anglo-Scottish struggle, trace the development of techniques of war and fortification, weaponry and architecture, give some account of the remarkable warrior-robber folk of the region, and provide a guide to the towers and castles, grim reminders of a turbulent past in a land of fairytale beauty.

George MacDonald Fraser,
historian and author of **The Steel Bonnets**, the story of the Anglo-Scottish Border Reivers.

Acknowledgements

This book was written, compiled and edited by John Dent and Rory McDonald of the Archaeology and Countryside Section, and designed by the Graphics Section of Scottish Borders Council, as part of the "Heritage Interpretation Project".

Scottish Borders Council is pleased to acknowledge financial support from the European Regional Development Fund and Scottish Natural Heritage which assisted in the production of this book.

We would like to thank the following people for their help and advice during the preparation of this book: Richard Allan, Chris Badenoch, Ian Brown, Rosamond Brown, Malcolm Clark, Louise Comrie, Ranald Dods, Doreen Grove, Ian King, Keith Robeson, Scottish Borders Council Museums Service, Scottish Borders Tourist Board.

Introduction

The historic border between England and Scotland was administered by Wardens of the Marches, and this book concerns those areas which fell within the Scottish Middle and East Marches. The shires of Selkirk, Roxburgh and Peebles made up the former, and Berwickshire made up the latter. Together, these shires have been known traditionally as "the Borders", and this name has endured through recent administrative changes, so that the region is today officially titled "Scottish Borders".

England is traditionally known as the "Auld Enemy" of Scotland and the two kingdoms were at war for much of the 14th, 15th and 16th centuries. Even so, although Berwick finally ended up on the English side of the Border in 1482, and the "Debateable Land" on the west was partitioned in 1552, no major changes have been made to the present border line since the 12th century.

Past armies left ruined abbeys and a ravaged landscape in their wake, and Borderers responded not only by turning their homes into fortresses, but also by carrying the war over the frontier hills. Reprisals led to vendettas and the spoils of war were replaced by peacetime plunder, as the frontier sank into the kind of lawlessness which is reminiscent of the American West, yet "Jeddart (Jedburgh) Justice" was a byword for summary execution long before the days of Judge Lynch.

The stage for these ancient dramas was the fertile valleys of the Tweed and Teviot, and the backdrop the wild Cheviot, Lammermuir, Tweedsmuir and Moorfoot Hills. The players were as colourful a mixture as could be hoped for: hardy Borderers with horse and lance and with everything to lose; ruthless politicians bent on power; Italian engineers and foreign mercenaries there for the money and adventure; pressed Scottish and English soldiers risking their lives because they had no choice. This is a landscape with a past which captivates the imagination, and this book helps Borderers and visitors to understand both the history and the sites which they may encounter in the landscape.

Please note, however, that mention of an archaeologically important site in the text does not indicate that it may be visited. The reader should be aware that although many sites are marked on Ordnance Survey maps or may be readily visible in the landscape, most are located on private land and are not generally accessible. At the end of the book the reader will find a list of those sites which are open to the public at the time of printing, those museums which contain collections of artefacts, and sources of further information.

Please remember, whenever visiting these sites, always follow the Country Code:

- Guard against all risk of fire
- Fasten all gates
- Keep dogs under close control
- Keep to paths across farmland
- Avoid damaging fences

- Leave no litter
- Safeguard water supplies
- Protect wildlife, wild plants and trees
- Go carefully on country roads
- Respect the life of the countryside

Table of Contents

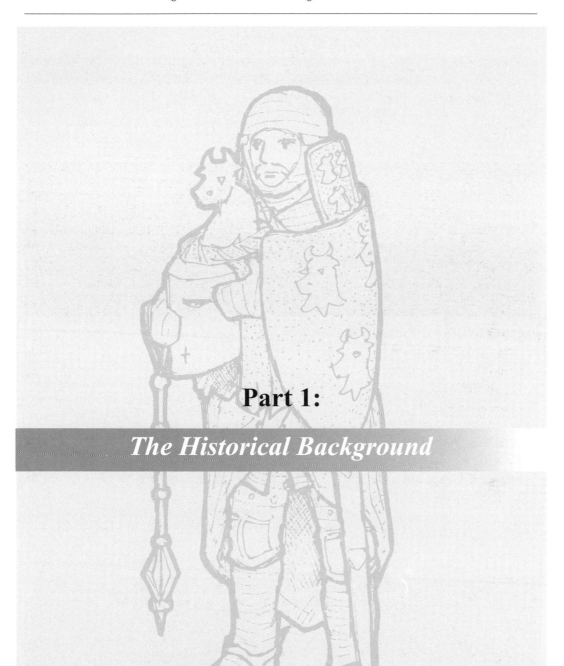

Part 1:

The Historical Background

Time Chart

Chronology	Events in the Borders	The Wider Picture
5th – 7th centuries Immigration Period.	603: The battle of Degsastan postpones expansion of the Scotti.	The Scotti extend Irish Dalriada to include the west coast; The Angli establish the kingdom of Bernicia, which later formed part of Northumbria, as far as the Forth.
8th – 13th centuries **Gradual consolidation of kingdoms.**	**760: The battle of Eildon establishes Aethelwold on the Bernician throne.** **1018: The battle of Carham confirms Scottish possession of lands as far as the River Tweed.** **12th century: Royal castles built at Berwick, Roxburgh, Jedburgh, Selkirk and Peebles.**	**Expansion of Dalriadan power to incorporate Pictland, Strathclyde and Lothian to the Tweed.** **Emergence of Scotland and England as political entities, with the national border between the Solway and Tweedmouth.** **Scottish involvement in English civil wars.**
1296-1357 Wars of Independence.	Royal castles change hands as fortunes wax and wane. 1297: William Wallace pursues the English to Hutton Moor after the battle of Stirling Bridge. 1304: Wallace defeated by an English raiding party at Happrew but continues a guerrilla war from Ettrick Forest. 1333: Berwick captured by the English after the battle of Halidon Hill. 1355: Franco-Scottish force defeated the English in a skirmish on Nisbet Moor. 1357: Treaty of Berwick.	Struggle for power following the death of Margaret, used to personal advantage by Edward I of England. John and Edward of Balliol supported by England; Robert and David of Bruce represent Scottish independence. Robert I defeats Edward II of England and carries the war into England. David II captured after the battle of Neville's Cross and held prisoner in England for eleven years, but still manages to conclude a peace with Edward III, who then makes no further attempt to conquer Scotland.
Later 14th – 15th centuries **Sporadic warfare.**	**1385: Melrose Abbey burnt by the English.** **1435: The Scots repel an English force at Piperdean.** **1460: Roxburgh Castle captured from the English and destroyed.**	**Hostilities with England maintained in an alliance with France.** **Border knights fight for France in the Hundred Years War.** **1482: Berwick captured and incorporated into England.**

Fig.1 Events relating to Border Warfare.

Chronology	Events in the Borders	The Wider Picture
16th century Further struggles to maintain Scotland's independence.	1522-3: The Earl of Surrey raids the Borders and sacks Jedburgh. 1526: A bid to capture the young king fails at Skirmish Field. 1542: English beaten at Hadden Rig. 1545: Scots victory at Ancrum Moor; Hertford's Raid devastates much of the Borders. 1547-57: The English and French build forts in Borders. 1559: The Treaty of Cateau-Cambrèsis concluded in Ladykirk Church. 1575: Redeswire Fray breaks out at Wardens' Meeting.	The marriage between James IV and Margaret Tudor is followed by the disaster at Flodden and the death of James (1513). There follows a power struggle for control of young James V. The death of James V (1542) leads to Anglo-French rivalry for the hand of the infant Queen Mary and the domination of Scotland. Sporadic civil war is driven by political and religious motives and linked to foreign intervention. This culminates in the Reformation (1560). Growing lawlessness in the Borderlands.
17th and 18th centuries **Bishops' Wars; Civil War.** **Jacobite risings.**	**1639: English and Scottish stand-off in Berwickshire.** **1645: The battle of Philiphaugh cuts short Royalist recruiting in the Borders.** **1715: The Jacobite standard is raised in Kelso.** **1745-6: Charles Edward Stuart in the Borders.**	**1603: The Union of Crowns removes the circumstances which favour border raiding.** **Charles I's policies antagonise large numbers of Scottish and English subjects.** **Establishment of permanent standing army.** **The Revolution of 1688 deposes James VII, but leads to later Jacobite bids for power from Scotland.** **1707: Act of Union between Scotland and England.**
19th and 20th centuries Imperial expansion and World Wars. Decline of the Empire.	The King's Own Scottish Borderers serve in many campaigns overseas. 1903: Stobs training camp established. 1914-18: Berwickshire airfields built. 1943: Charlesfield munitions factory opens.	Head start in agricultural and industrial growth initially provides the basis for a world-wide empire, policed by the Royal Navy and British Army. Global conflicts involve the whole population, followed by the loss of the empire and a much reduced need for substantial armed forces.

Part 1: The Historical Background

Development of a border

During the latter part of the 4th century AD Britain south of Hadrian's Wall was ruled as part of the Roman Empire and what is now the Borders lay well to the north in what may be termed "Independent Britain". The Imperial provinces came under increasing pressure from the free kingdoms of the north and from raiders who came by ship from Ireland and from across the North Sea. In the early years of the 5th century the Romans withdrew from Britain and created a "power vacuum" in which the former provinces broke up into a series of independent kingdoms.

Between the 5th and 11th centuries Britain underwent a gradual process of political centralisation, by which the small kingdoms were absorbed into larger ones. During this period the native Britons struggled to preserve their independence and their language (which only survives as modern Welsh) against increasing settlement by Gaelic-speaking *Scotti* of *Dalriada* (a kingdom which included much of north-east Ireland as well as Scotland's west coast) and English-speaking *Angli* (**fig.2**).

Although the legendary British hero King Arthur has mythical associations with the Eildon Hills, an early Welsh epic poem describes a real war band of *Gododdin* and their heroic ride from Din Eiddyn (Edinburgh) to Catraeth (Catterick) in Yorkshire, where they died in battle against the Angli. These riders would have passed through the Borders and along the Roman road, Dere Street, which continued to have a strategic importance and

Language and the Border

Scottish Borders
Anglo-Scottish Border
Gaelic name with "baile"
Anglian name with "ham" or "ingtun"

0   100 kilometres   0   100 miles

Fig.2 *The distribution of settlement names including "baile" (Gaelic) and "ham" and "ingtun" (English) shows how the Scotti and Angli came to dominate the natives of northern Britain between the 5th and the 7th centuries. The boundary between the two groups remained fluid for several centuries until Scotland and England emerged as independent states, each under its own king.*

influenced where armies marched and battles were fought.

The Anglian kingdom of *Bernicia* (which later became part of Northumbria) extended into the Borders in the course of the 6th and 7th centuries. Its border with the Britons of *Strathclyde* may have been marked, in Teviotdale, by the Catrail. This was a boundary made up of intermittent linear earthworks (as well as ridges, streams and perhaps woods which are no longer there), which separated the arable lowlands of the east from the less fertile uplands of the west.

King Aethelfrith of Bernicia defeated King Áedán mac Gabhráin of Dalriada in AD603 at Degsastan (usually identified as Dawston in Liddesdale). In the century which followed this battle, Lothian, which at that time included all the area between the Forth and the Tweed, came under the power of the Anglian kings of Northumbria. Many settlement names survive from that time and those which once ended in *ham* (such as Oxnam, Ednam, Edrom and Coldingham) or *ceastr* (such as Bonchester (Hobkirk), Belchester (Eccles) and Rowchester (Bowden)) represent Anglian homesteads or forts of the period.

Although the Angles ventured beyond the Forth into the land of the Picts (where King Ecgfrith of Northumbria was killed in battle at Nechtansmere in AD685), it was the successors of Áedán mac Gabhráin who came to rule both the Scotti and the Picts as the single kingdom of *Alba*. Among the hills of the western Borders are many places with names which recall the native Britons, as well as some which derive from the Irish language. Native are names such as Cardrona (Traquair), Carlops (West Linton), Caerlee (Innerleithen: *caer* = "fort"), Peebles (*pebyll* = "tent") and Traquair (*tref quair* = "the settlement on the river Quair"). In the Tweedsmuir Hills Irish speaking incomers from the west called many of the valleys "glens", as Glenwhappen (Tweedsmuir), Glengaber (Yarrow), Glenrath (Manor) and other valleys bear witness. Kilbucho (Broughton) takes its name from the Gaelic for chapel of St Bee (*cille begha*) which stood there from early Christian times.

King Kenneth mac Alpin launched several attacks on Anglian Lothian, in the course of which he sacked the Northumbrian monastery of Old Melrose in AD859. These and subsequent assaults on the region brought it under Scottish occupation, although it was not finally secured from the English kingdom until King Malcolm II's victory over Earl Ughtred of Northumbria at Carham (Northumberland) on the Tweed in or about 1018. Henceforward, with only minor interruption, the lower Tweed would mark the eastern end of the border between the newly emerging kingdoms of Scotland and England.

Feudalism and overlordship

Feudalism was a social system, introduced to Britain by the Normans of Northern France, in which a piece of land (*a fief*) was held as part of a close mutual bond between a liege lord and his tenant or *vassal*. This bond could be between the king and one of his nobles, or between a noble and one of his free tenants. The terms of the agreement imposed obligations on both lord and vassal. One feature of the system was that a fief was not rented in the modern sense but the occupying vassal provided his liege lord with services in kind. Military service was particularly important because it allowed the king to raise a feudal army from his vassals and their supporters. King David I introduced the system and granted lands to Norman knights from England to encourage Scotland's development. The first earthwork castles, (such as the Lovel family's *motte* and *bailey* at Hawick: **fig.3 & Plate 3**) were erected by these Norman nobles, partly for their protection and partly as a mark of their social position.

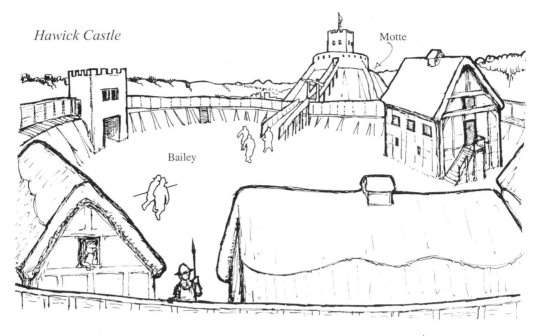

Fig.3 *Hawick Castle, home of the Lovel family, as it might have appeared in the 13th century.*

The Norman nobility could have land in Scotland, England and France and thus be subjects of three kings. The Balliol family, for example, had estates in Teviotdale, in County Durham, and around Bailleul in Normandy. This even extended to the monarchs themselves. In the 12th century David I was also Earl of Huntingdon, in which role he was a vassal of the English crown. After 1066 the Norman kings of England were themselves vassals of the French crown in respect of their continental lands and this was a root cause of the wars between England and France in the later 13th, 14th and 15th centuries.

Subservience to a foreign ruler for lands abroad must have been irksome to medieval kings, but to have a neighbouring monarch claim overlordship for no better reason than his greater power and wealth was intolerable.

The book known as the Anglo-Saxon Chronicle claims that in AD927 King Constantine II of Alba recognised King Athelstan of *Wessex* as his overlord in return for control of Lothian. William the Conqueror and other medieval English kings used this as the basis of claims to superiority over Scottish kings, which were for the most part firmly resisted.

Overlordship was a diplomatic bargaining tool, along with dynastic marriage. The Scottish and English royal houses were regularly linked by marriage. David I and King Henry I were brothers-in-law; so were later kings such as Alexander III and Edward I and James IV and Henry VIII. No doubt these marriages were arranged with a view to the eventual union of the royal houses, which finally came about in 1603 with the accession of King James VI to the throne of England.

The Borders in the Wars of Independence

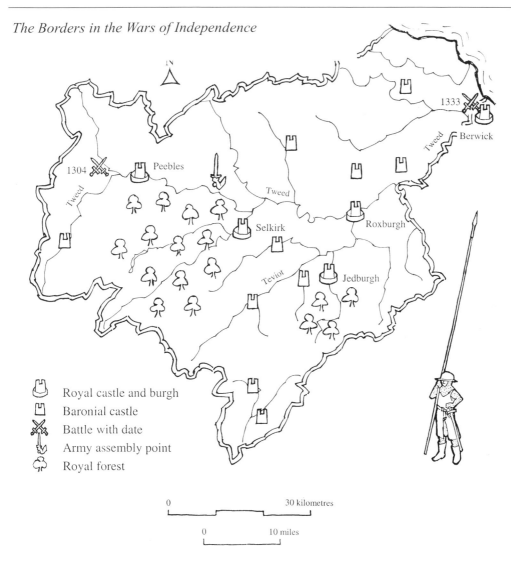

Fig.4 *In the wars of the late 13*[th] *and 14*[th] *centuries the castles of the Borders played a key role, and changed hands on several occasions. The royal forests provided a secure retreat for guerrilla fighters led by William Wallace and others. Although few battles were fought in the region, the area was ravaged by invading armies on many occasions.*

The Border Wars

King David I intervened in the English civil wars of the 12th century with the intention of obtaining England's northernmost counties (Cumberland had been Scottish before 1092). In this he was successful and for more than ten years Scotland's southern boundary lay between the mouth of the River Tees and Morecambe Bay. These territories reverted to the English king, Henry II, who for a time also held the Borders castles of Jedburgh, Roxburgh (across the Tweed from present day Kelso) and Berwick.

King William the Lion also involved himself in England's internal affairs and was captured at Alnwick in 1174 in an attempt to regain the Earldom of Northumberland, which his grandfather had held as a vassal of the English king. His son, King Alexander II not only allowed fugitive English barons to seek safety in Scotland but received their homage in the Chapter House of Melrose Abbey, for which he was rewarded by King John with an invasion of Lothian and the sack of Coldingham Priory in 1216.

The greater part of the 13th century saw peace between the two kingdoms and the Scottish claim to England's northernmost counties was finally abandoned by Alexander II in the Treaty of York in 1237. His son and namesake was more concerned with defeating the Norwegians who occupied much of the north and west coasts. King Alexander III's victory and the death of King Haakon IV at Largs in 1263 were decisive and united Scotland under his rule. However, more than twenty years later his achievements were thrown into jeopardy when, in his haste to join his young bride, he plunged over a cliff in Fife in 1286. This and the early death of his young daughter Margaret four years later, set the scene for a long and bitter struggle, as three generations of English kings, all called Edward, set out to extend their control over their northern neighbour.

In the Wars of Independence which followed, Scottish nobility was usually divided into pro- and anti-English parties (many nobles still had lands in England) and this in itself was cause for civil war. King Edward I had negotiated a treaty at Birgham (Eccles) near Coldstream, by which his son would unite the Scottish and

English houses through marriage to Margaret. Now he took advantage over Scotland's weakness to apply pressure to Margaret's successor, King John (of the House of Balliol) and make him compliant to his will. Although John is often regarded as Edward's puppet, it was his defiance of the English king which led to his defeat and deposition in 1296 and the loss of the Scottish crown jewels, the Stone of Destiny and the royal Border castles of Berwick, Roxburgh and Jedburgh **(fig.4)**.

During this period Scottish resistance stiffened under William Wallace, who defeated an English army at Stirling Bridge in 1297 and was named "Guardian of the Realm", reputedly in Selkirk church **(fig.5)**. Following

Fig.5 Heroic William Wallace sustained Scottish resistance to English domination after the capture of King John. Ettrick Forest was the base for his guerrilla war, and his statue at Bemersyde was erected in 1814 by the Earl of Buchan.

his own defeat at Falkirk in 1298, Wallace turned to guerrilla warfare, in which he used the extensive forests of Selkirk, Ettrick and Traquair as a refuge. Partly to guard against attack from this direction, Edward I built a *"pele"* at Selkirk in 1301-2 on the site of the earlier castle. This was captured by the Scots in 1302 and held for almost a decade.

Wallace's victories (and his brutal death in 1305) are the stuff of legend but it was Robert Bruce, Earl of Carrick and claimant to the crown of Scotland, who now assumed leadership of the resistance movement and developed Wallace's guerrilla tactics to achieve eventual success. The Scottish nobility and clergy rallied to Bruce's support and he was crowned King Robert I in 1306. Edward I, worn out after numerous campaigns in France, Wales and Scotland, finally died at Burgh-on-Sands (Cumbria) while on his way north for yet another campaign in 1307.

Robert I worked hard to unite his subjects but King Edward II of England managed to alienate his own supporters with little effort and brought his army to humiliating defeat at Bannockburn in 1314, after which he was unable to control Scottish incursions into England. Robert's armies penetrated southwards into Yorkshire and Lancashire and almost captured Edward himself at Byland (Yorkshire) in 1322. The English king proved himself incapable of protecting his northern subjects, many of whom paid the Scots to be left alone.

The royal castles of Berwick, Roxburgh and Jedburgh were key strongholds and enabled English troops to continue to dominate Teviotdale and lower Tweeddale, except when the castles themselves were under attack. When fighting on the defensive, Robert preferred to destroy castles rather than allow them to fall into hands of the enemy. One exception to this rule was Roxburgh which was captured by "Good Sir James" Douglas before Bannockburn and held by the Scots for a time, although it was ultimately destroyed in 1460.

Douglas was one of Robert I's great captains and a product of the wars. He acquired great influence in the Borders, where he was granted the confiscated lands of pro-English barons such as the Soules of Liddesdale and Comyns of Bedrule. His kinsmen extended this influence to make the "Black Douglases" the most powerful family in the south of Scotland during the 14th and early 15th centuries. Their properties in the Borders included the castles of Hermitage (Castleton), Cavers and Newark (Selkirk) and Drumlanrig's Tower (Hawick).

In 1320 it was another Borderer, Bernard of Linton who, as Abbot of the Tironensian monastery of Arbroath, drafted the stirring Declaration of Arbroath, which states:

> *"for so long as a hundred of us remain alive, we will never in any way be bowed beneath the yoke of English domination; for it is not for glory, riches or honour that we fight, but for freedom alone, that which no man of worth yields up, save with his life".*

Robert I not only frustrated further English attempts on Scottish soil but he also carried the war far into England. By his death in 1329 he had concluded the Treaty of Edinburgh-Northampton by which the young King Edward III of England recognised Scottish independence **(fig.6)**. He also raised Scotland's prestige as a European nation, although his alliance with France in 1326 was to embroil his country in Anglo-French wars and lead, in time, to the disasters of Neville's Cross (1346) and Flodden (1513).

Treaties

- **Treaty of York (1237)** between Alexander II of Scotland and Henry III of England set the boundary between the two kingdoms broadly on its present line, and the former gave up his claim to the northern counties of England.

- **Treaty of Birgham (1290)** arranged the betrothal of the young Queen Margaret to the Prince of Wales, son of King Edward I of England, who agreed with the guardians of her realm that Scotland would remain a separate kingdom.

- **Treaty of Edinburgh-Northampton (1328)** declared the young King Edward III's recognition of King Robert I as the king of Scotland and abandoned claims of English overlordship.

- **Treaty of Berwick (1357)** called a truce between England and Scotland and secured the release of King David II, who had been a prisoner of war since his capture at the Battle of Neville's Cross in 1346.

- **Treaty of Boulogne (1550)** between England and France led to the removal of garrisons and dismantling of English forts at Eyemouth, Lauder and Roxburgh.

- **Treaty of Cateau Cambrésis (1559)** ended sixty-five years of hostilities between France and Spain and included their respective allies, Scotland and England. This treaty brought about the destruction of the French fort at Eyemouth.

Fig.6 *Treaties*

Robert I's heart was buried in Melrose Abbey after being carried to the *Crusades* by Sir James Douglas but the king's death led to a period of further warfare. His son, King David II was only five years old, which encouraged the heir of John to assert his own claim to the throne. King Edward was crowned at Scone in 1332 and was supported by nobles whose family lands had been confiscated by Robert I. He was kept in place by Edward III of England, to whom he granted the Borders, Lothian and Dumfriesshire and acknowledged as overlord.

This situation was intolerable, not only to most Scots but also to the French. After a crushing defeat at Halidon Hill (Northumberland; 1333) which resulted in the capture of Berwick, the supporters of David II (who was in France for his safety) reverted to guerrilla warfare and Edward III soon tired of costly campaigns without result. Moreover, war with France was to dominate English foreign policy from 1337 to 1453.

Civil war between the supporters of David II (who returned to Scotland in 1341) and Edward (heavily supported by English troops) continued until after David's invasion of England, and his defeat and capture at Neville's Cross. Although David was taken into captivity (which would last for eleven years) by the end of 1347 support for the Balliol cause had effectively vanished from Scotland.

In 1355 a Scottish force routed an English force on Nisbet Moor (Edrom) and in the following year, while some Scots were fighting the English in France, David II's supporters captured Berwick. This provoked Edward III to inflict a devastation on south-east Scotland which is still remembered as the "Burnt Candlemas". While the English king was at Roxburgh, he witnessed King Edward's dramatic renunciation of his claim to the Scottish throne. By the Treaty of Berwick (1357) David II was released and a truce was signed between Scotland and England which was to last for twenty-seven years, although the key fortresses of Berwick, Roxburgh and Jedburgh remained in English hands.

French troops were directly involved in the next stage of the war, which was revived in 1385. By this time, Robert Stewart had succeeded his uncle, David, as King Robert II, while King Richard II was on the throne of England. The war opened with Richard's invasion of the Borders and Lothian. The ruined abbey church of Melrose is a lasting memorial of the devastation carried out during this conflict. A Franco-Scottish invasion of England followed and in 1388 the Scots were victorious at Otterburn (Northumberland) although their leader, James Douglas, Earl of Douglas and Mar, was killed.

George Dunbar, the Earl of March, defected to the English side in 1400 in reaction to a slight by King Robert III and he or his son defeated a Scottish raiding force at West Nisbet (Langton) in 1402. March joined the Earl of Northumberland and his son, Henry "Hotspur" Percy, in the victory of Homildon Hill (Northumberland) in 1402. Hotspur then laid siege to Cocklaw Castle (Hawick) which formed part of those Douglas estates supposedly granted to the Percys by the English king Henry IV.

The deaths of Hotspur and his uncle at Shrewsbury in 1403 and the Earl of Northumberland at Bramham Moor in 1408, in rebellion against their king, removed for a time the threat which the Percy family had long represented to the Borders. Jedburgh Castle was finally recaptured by the men of Teviotdale and demolished (at a cost of two pence per household throughout Scotland) in 1409 to avoid its use by the English. Henry IV was the last reigning English king to lead an army into Scotland and his son King Henry V turned his attention to campaigns in France.

Henry V was accompanied in these wars by King James I of Scotland, who had been taken prisoner, aged twelve, on his way back from France in 1406. Among the Scots who fought, and died, on the French side were the Border lords John Swinton and Archibald Douglas. The son of George Dunbar, however, continued to harbour a grudge against his sovereign, and with an English force from Berwick was defeated at Piperdean (Northumberland) in 1435.

The 'Wars of the Roses' in England (1455-85) provided an opportunity for King James III to recapture the two castles which had remained in English hands. In 1460 he was killed by an exploding cannon while besieging Roxburgh but the castle fell to his queen, Mary of Gueldres. In the following year the fugitive King Henry VI of England handed over Berwick but it was recaptured by the Duke of Gloucester (later King Richard III) in 1482 and has been detached from Scotland ever since.

During this period, the Scots and English watched their royal families and nobility squabble over the crown and even plot with national enemies. It is unsurprising, therefore, to find that families on both sides of the border regarded the idea of patriotism with cynicism and preferred to follow their own judgement and self-interest. During the 16th century in particular, the Scottish and English marches became notorious for the lawlessness among its inhabitants, who were a constant thorn in the sides of the authorities. *Reiving*, or robbery, became a way of life, as did kidnapping and enforced protection money. The words "gang" and "blackmail" originated on the frontier at this time, and grievances between families were kept alive for generations. Although the authorities did their best to control and suppress this lawlessness, they also made good use of the Borderers as light horsemen whenever it was convenient to do so.

Although King James IV married Margaret (the sister of King Henry VIII of England) he nonetheless honoured his obligations to his French allies when Henry invaded France in 1513. James, in turn, invaded England and was killed, along with much of Scotland's nobility. The Battle of Flodden (Northumberland) which took place only a few miles south of the Tweed, was the worst military disaster in Scottish history. The English were too weak to follow up their victory, however, and an English force of over 4,000 under Lord Dacre was defeated two months later at Sclaterford Bridge (Hobkirk/ Southdean).

France had bolstered Scotland's forces with her own troops in the past and the alliance saw more Frenchmen take part in the wars of the 16th century. This was not a constant blessing,

however, for in the fighting of 1522-3, when the Borders was being devastated by the English under Lord Dacre and the Earl of Surrey, French troops are reported to have caused more damage to Scottish property than the English.

During these years the Border Reivers were particularly active to the point that even Lord Dacre complained to the Scottish King that the Elliots, Nixons, Croziers and Armstrongs were ambushing and killing his servants while on their lawful business. In 1530 King James V descended on the Borders with 8,000 and hanged fifty men including the famous reiver, Johnie Armstrong at Caerlanrig (Teviothead).

In 1538 James V cemented the alliance with France through his marriage with Mary of Guise. Thereafter, his relationship with his uncle Henry deteriorated rapidly. His death of "nervous exhaustion" following his army's humiliating defeat at Solway Moss in 1542 brought his newly born daughter, Mary to the throne. Her great-uncle Henry of England devised a plan to secure the Scottish throne for his young son, Edward, by a dynastic marriage between the two. When his diplomacy failed, he resorted to war, and in this *"Rough Wooing"* the people of the Border country suffered time and time again.

Through his conflict with France Henry found himself in alliance with Charles V (Holy Roman Emperor and King of Spain) and this enabled him to field a combined army of English, Welsh, Irish, Spanish, Italian, German and Balkan troops. Opposing these were Scots, supported by French soldiers. The fighting of the 1540s continued after Henry's death and through most of the next decade.

Hertford's Raid of September 1545

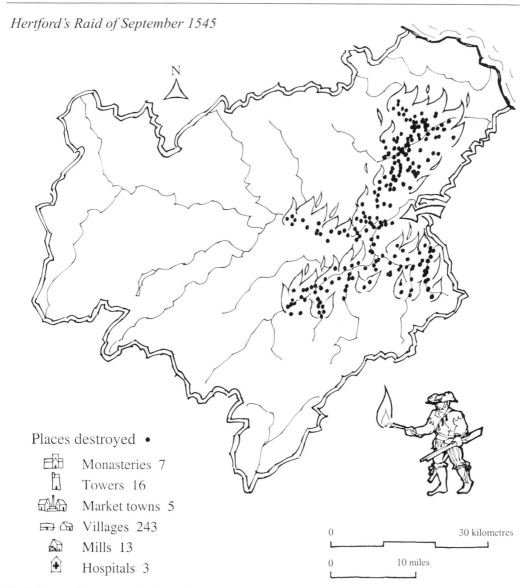

Places destroyed •

Monasteries 7

Towers 16

Market towns 5

Villages 243

Mills 13

Hospitals 3

Fig.7 *Places "burnt, razed and cast down" by the army of the Earl of Hertford in 1545.*

During this period the Borders must have seen and heard an exotic mixture of dress and speech.

This was a hard time for the Borders, as Henry did not want to acquire land but rather to devastate large areas of southern Scotland. His armies with the support of the English fleet, passed through the Borders and left behind garrisons at Roxburgh, Hume, Eyemouth, Lauder and Ferniehirst (Jedburgh). Although these were desperate times for the Scots they did have some victories, notably at the Battle of Ancrum Moor (1545). Joy at this victory was brief for later in that year the Earl of Hertford invaded, putting most of the Merse and Teviotdale to the flame **(fig.7)**. To further strengthen their position the English constructed artillery forts at Lauder, Eyemouth, Roxburgh and Dunglass (East Lothian). These were short-lived, however, as they were handed over for demolition under the Treaty of Boulogne. The fort at Eyemouth was refortified briefly by the French in 1557 and this prompted the English queen Mary to embark on a reconstruction of the walls of Berwick. Ultimately, however, Eyemouth was abandoned under the terms of the Treaty of Cateau Cambrèsis, the final part of which was signed in the church of our Lady of the Steill at Ladykirk in 1559.

The English queen Elizabeth I maintained a truce with Scotland and in general this was kept, although the armed commotion known as the Redeswire Fray (1575) developed from what should have been a peaceful meeting of the Wardens of the March on the Border at Carter Bar (Jedburgh/ Southdean). Wardens' meetings were regular events to hear and redress grievances against reivers. They met with limited success, for the Wardens were often unable to enforce the Border Law (the *Leges Marchiarum* specially devised for the frontier), and some of them were sadly inefficient; a few were ready to wink at wrongdoing, or even work in league with the reivers **(fig.8)**.

Union and thereafter

Queen Elizabeth I of England never married and her cousin, King James VI, inherited her throne in 1603. By this time, reiving had become an established way of life for many on both sides of the border. James took steps to suppress this activity, which was detrimental to both his kingdoms and gave many former reivers the task of hunting down and hanging

Wardens of the Marches

The borderland, or marches, on both sides of the frontier were divided into an East, Middle and West March, and each was administered by a Warden who was responsible for maintaining law and order in his area during peacetime, and for commanding it in time of war. Liddesdale was so lawless and isolated that it had its own Keeper, who assisted the Warden of the Scottish Middle March.

The Scottish Wardens were usually appointed from powerful local families, and outsiders could be resented. None, it would seem, more than Anthony Darcy, a Frenchman who was murdered in 1516 by kinsmen of Lord Home, the previous Warden of the East March. Having killed him, they took his head to Duns for display in the market place.

Some Borders officials have passed into literature and folklore. In 1566 Queen Mary made a celebrated visit to Hermitage Castle where the Keeper of Liddesdale, her lover the Earl of Bothwell, was recovering from an encounter with the local Elliot family. Another Keeper, Walter Scott known as the "Bold Buccleuch", created a sensation in 1596 when he liberated a notorious reiver, Kinmont Willie Armstrong, in a night raid on Carlisle Castle.

Many Wardens on both sides were corrupt, but were tolerated by higher authority if they kept order on the frontier. Tweeddale and Teviotdale suffered most at the hands of English Wardens, such as Thomas, Lord Dacre who led some devastating raids in the years after the Battle of Flodden, and Ralph Eure, whose career was ended at Ancrum Moor in 1545.

Cross-border justice was the business of Warden Meetings, when cases of reiving, kidnapping and blackmail were judged. Vested interests often resulted in bad judgements, and meetings could get out of hand. The Redeswire Fray broke out during a meeting near Carter Bar in 1575, and Lord Francis Russell was murdered at another, at Windy Gyle (Morebattle), in 1585.

Fig.8 Wardens of the Marches

their erstwhile accomplices and other wrongdoers. This concerted effort took effect but in 1637 there were still thirty-seven executions. General lawlessness continued in the chaos of the religious and civil wars of the late 1630s and 40s and during the religious persecution of the later 17th century known as the "Killing Times". This period was still recalled in oral tradition into the 20th century. In the Cheviot Hills, thieves known as "mosstroopers" remained active after the suppression of the reiving families by James VI, and construction of fortified homes continued by those who were yet to be convinced that peaceful times had arrived.

Although continued hostility was difficult to sustain when one king ruled both nations, King Charles I did his best in his two military adventures to impose the Church of England on the Scots (the so-called "Bishops' Wars" of 1639-40). Moreover, he divided society in the two countries so successfully that both were torn by civil wars in the 1640s.

Charles' opponents in the "Bishops' Wars" were Covenanters – supporters of the revolutionary document known as the National Covenant, which denounced Roman Catholicism and the tendency of Charles' policies in that direction, while at the same time it asserted the power and rights of the elected parliament. In 1639, Covenanting forces camped on Duns Law which they fortified with earthworks, while Charles' troops camped on the south bank of the Tweed. His troops crossed the river via a bridge of boats which was guarded by fortifications on the site of Paxton House (Hutton). This first confrontation was relatively bloodless and concluded in the Peace of Berwick, which was so unsatisfactory that in the following year the Covenanters invaded England and forced Charles to concede to their demands.

The Covenanters proved to be natural allies to the Parliamentary side in the English Civil War and although this widened to Scotland in 1644, the lack of royalist support in the Borders meant that most of the fighting took place further north, where the Marquis of Montrose won a dazzling series of victories for the king. Montrose travelled to the Borders in an attempt to raise support for Charles, but met with opposition and was routed at the Battle of Philiphaugh (Selkirk) on 13 September 1645. Victory for Parliament in the English Civil War was followed by the execution of the king in 1649.

His son, the future King Charles II, gained support in Scotland, which provoked invasion and conquest by a force under Oliver Cromwell in 1650. Cromwell battered Coldingham Priory with artillery and decisively defeated Leslie's army at Dunbar. His men were quartered throughout the Borders in the towns and villages where the inhabitants were obliged to provide them with food and shelter. This led to a great deal of hardship and poverty for many of the communities until 1660, when General Monck led a force from Coldstream in support of Charles II. This force, consisting of the remnants of Fenwick's and Hesselrigg's regiments, was re-organised and subsequently became known as the Coldstream Guards in recognition of its participation in the Restoration of the Monarchy. The story of the regiment is told at the museum which stands on the site of the house which was Monck's headquarters.

Charles II was more successful than his father in imposing the Church of England on his Scottish subjects and Covenanters found their religion proscribed until the Glorious Revolution of 1688. This policy had important implications in the Borders, where open air "conventicles" were harshly suppressed and rough justice handed out by the authorities to the likes of John Hunter, "murdered" and buried at Tweedsmuir.

The "Revolution" of 1688, which replaced King James VII with William of Orange, was welcomed in the Borders but not in the Highlands. The new king authorised the Earl of Leven to raise a regiment of 800 foot soldiers to protect his interests in Scotland, which they attempted to do soon afterwards at the Battle of Killiecrankie (Perthshire). In spite of the regiment's efforts, the royal army was defeated. This regiment subsequently became the 25th Regiment of Foot and later the King's Own Scottish Borderers, which has for much of its life been based at Berwick upon Tweed.

The Parliaments of Scotland and England were amalgamated by the Act of Union of 1707 and thereafter Scotland had no separate administration until the new Scottish Parliament came into being in 1999. As part of the United Kingdom, the Borders contributed soldiers to the new British Army and until recent re-organisation of the armed forces this contribution was consistently more than twice the national Scottish average.

The new army not only served in foreign wars and in the defence of the growing British Empire but was also used to suppress unrest at home. Leven's Regiment took part in the battles of Sheriffmuir (1715) and Culloden (1746) against the supporters of the *Old Pretender* and *Bonnie Prince Charlie*, in their bids to regain the crown for the House of Stuart. In 1715 the Jacobite standard was raised at Kelso Cross, while in 1745-6, rebels stayed at Thirlestane Castle (Lauder) and Traquair House. Although the Jacobite uprisings saw the last battles to take place on British soil, troops from the Borders fought in many subsequent conflicts, including the Seven Years War, the American War of Independence, the Napoleonic, Crimean and Boer Wars, the two World Wars, in Korea and more recently in the Arabian Gulf.

By the Second World War men and women were serving in the armed forces, and the civilian population also contributed to the war effort. Stobs Camp (Cavers) contained 100,000 soldiers at a time, Royal Air Force airfields existed at Charterhall (Eccles/ Fogo) and Whinfield (Hutton/ Whitsome) and Charlesfield (St Boswells) was the site of a major munitions factory in 1943-5.

Part 2:

How Wars were Fought

Part 2: How Wars were Fought

With the passage of time and the rise in population, the scale of warfare and its impact has increased. In the 6th century AD, the defeat of 300 Gododdin warriors was celebrated in an epic poem. In 1296, just one contingent of King Edward I's invasion force numbered 3,157 men when it joined the rest of his army at Roxburgh. In the 20th century 8,211 Borderers lost their lives in two World Wars and 24,633 were wounded. In addition to the much larger numbers of servicemen who escaped injury, in modern wars a substantial proportion of the civilian population has contributed to the war effort, particularly as Home Guard, fire fighters, munitions workers and air-raid wardens.

This increase in scale has kept pace with changes in the character of warfare. After the collapse of the Roman Empire, medieval society lacked the organisation and resources to maintain permanent armies of professional soldiers. In the power struggles which developed between the emerging kingdoms of the post-Roman centuries, social and military leadership were inseparable and an aristocracy developed from capable warriors supported by a nucleus of chosen men.

As early medieval societies stabilised, warriors were rewarded with land, a process which developed into the feudal system. Under this system land and protection were provided, in return for military service, directly from the king, or from one of his feudal tenant. Feudalism created mutual bonds between the leaders and the led, who met as an armed host at *weaponshaws*.

The feudal armies which Edward the I brought to Scotland were raised on the basis of an obligation to provide forty days military service in the year. Once this period was over, the soldiers returned to their homes. Clearly this was only of value for short military campaigns, and during the 14th century there was an increasing tendency for feudal obligations to be commuted to goods or cash payments instead. Armed with this source of revenue it became possible to pay soldiers to fight for longer periods and a class of experienced warrior emerged. Such soldiers had the advantage that, even in smaller numbers, they were more effective fighters than the feudal host.

The Borders produced many notable examples, some of whom gained renown outwith Scotland. The Berwickshire knight, Sir John Swinton was one such soldier, who fought (and died) on behalf of his king's French allies in the early 15th century. The French chronicler Jean Froissart regarded several of the members of the powerful Douglas family as models of knightly prowess. From "Good Sir James" onwards, their skills on the battlefield were held in high regard at home and on the continent, especially in France.

During this period the basic weapons of the soldier were the sword, spear, axe and shield. Battles were decided on the outcome of hand-to-hand struggles. The mounted knight had dominated the battlefield since the fall of the Roman Empire but in the course of the Wars of Independence, the superiority of the aristocratic knight on horseback was challenged by common foot soldiers and cavalry lost their dominance of the battlefield.

14th-15th Century Arms and Armour

a   b   c   d

Fig.9 Soldiers of the medieval wars: (a) William Turnbull in chain mail armour of c.1315 with heraldic shield, helm and mace; (b) a foot soldier of c.1315 with helmet and claymore (Gaelic claidheumh mór = "great sword"); (c) Sir John Swinton c.1420 in plate armour with heraldic jupon, or surcoat; (d) foot soldier of c.1480 wearing a brigandine or "jack", salade helmet and carrying a Jedburgh stave.

Scottish infantry showed at Stirling Bridge and Bannockburn, that dense formations of men with pikes could resist horsemen, while at Falkirk and Halidon Hill English archers showed that arrows could kill men at a distance, whether they were on horseback or on foot and regardless of their social position.

More revolutionary than these weapons, however, was the introduction of gunpowder to the battlefield. Between the 14th and the 17th centuries the development of cannon and hand guns slowly changed the whole nature of warfare. Traditional fortifications were vulnerable to cannon fire, as was found by the defenders of Roxburgh Castle in 1460. *Gunloops* replaced arrow loops, and stone walls gave way to earthen ramparts. Bows and arrows continued to be used until late in the 16th century but were gradually replaced by the musket, and armour was still worn during the Civil Wars. By the end of the 17th century, professional soldiers resembled modern armies more than they resembled the feudal host of the Middle Ages. These soldiers dressed alike and were equipped with firearms and wheeled artillery.

Medieval warfare

The two major periods of trouble which affected the Borders most were the Wars of Independence and the Rough Wooing. These conflicts give two views of the soldiers, their weapons and the ways in which they used them. The first saw the bow and arrow begin to alter the social balance of power on the battlefield, and the second took place at a stage when gunpowder had brought into being a new type of professional soldier with a more scientific approach to war **(fig.9)**.

Dress

Although the range of weapons available to medieval soldiers included various forms of bow, as well as larger engines which could hurl projectiles hundreds of metres, most fighting consisted of hand-to-hand combat using a range of sharp or blunt tools. For this reason, soldiers took special interest in how they dressed for battle and took precautions to minimise risks to their own personal safety. Body armour was common, although this would necessarily reflect the purse of the wearer. When King Edward I mustered his forces at Roxburgh in 1298, they included some 10,900 Welsh and 14,800 English infantry, as well as a force of men-at-arms which probably numbered about 2,000. This suggests that only one out of every ten or fifteen soldiers is likely to have been heavily armoured.

Thick padding was a useful insurance, not only against bruising from blunt instruments but also against edged weapons which had been blunted in battle. Boiled leather was reasonably cheap and provided some protection, especially when studded with metal plates to make a padded jacket or *brigandine*. Chain mail had been known in Britain since the 2nd or 3rd century BC and was worn as full body armour by the mounted knights who met at Roxburgh in 1296. In the course of the next century or so, complete chain mail gave way gradually to steel plate, a transition which would have been complete by the time of the siege of Roxburgh in 1460.

A shield was worn on the left arm to provide additional protection, particularly in the days before plate armour replaced chain mail.

Knights carried long shields to cover much of the body, whereas a smaller round shield, known as *targe* or *buckler*, was carried by foot soldiers. Shields were made of wood toughened with a covering of leather or metal plate.

Many foot soldiers in the feudal levy would have lacked armour and no doubt relied on their innate nimbleness to avoid injury, whereas heavily armoured knights would have been severely restricted in their movement. To the mounted knights, these foot soldiers were amateurs in war and certainly not suitable opponents in hand-to-hand fighting. Warfare involved a good deal of ritual (which was developed in peacetime tournaments and jousts) and encouraged by the literature of chivalry.

The heavily armoured knights led their own contingents and were the rallying points for their followers in battle. Large protective helmets covered their faces and so to identify himself, each knight adopted an heraldic device as his personal emblem. This device would be displayed on the cloth *surcoat* which he wore over his armour, on his personal flag or banner, and on his shield **(fig.10)**. Some arms were simple geometric shapes, often derived from the reinforcing bands of shields, while others used martial figures such as the lion or the eagle. As the number of coats of arms grew it became necessary for special heralds to catalogue them, to avoid two people using the same combination of colours and features. The heraldic law is still enforced to this day by the Lord Lyon, King of Arms.

Heraldry in Battle c.1320

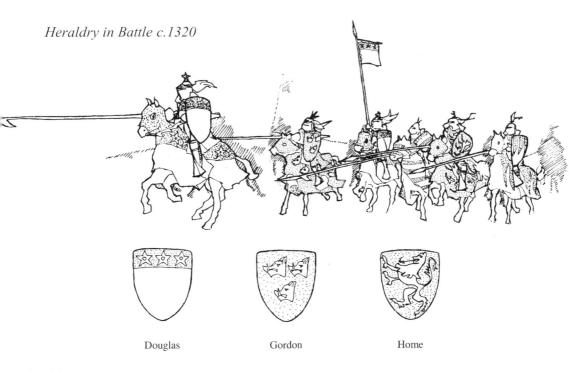

Douglas   Gordon   Home

Fig.10 *A distinctive coat of arms enabled medieval knights to recognise each other in battle, when their faces were covered by armour. They also marked out the wearers as gentlemen who could afford to pay a ransom if captured. Some foot soldiers wore the arms of their national saint to distinguish which side they were on.*

Equipment

The followers of a particular knight might have worn a badge to show their allegiance to him. St. Andrew was first adopted by Angus, King of the Picts in the 8th or 9th century after his cross was seen in the sky during a decisive battle. When the Pictish kingdom was amalgamated with Dalriada to form the Scottish kingdom of Alba, St. Andrew was adopted as Scotland's patron saint, and medieval heralds ascribed to him a coat of arms comprising a white saltire on a blue background. St. George was adopted as the patron saint of England, and his badge, a red cross on a white background, appeared on banners and was worn by English soldiers.

In addition to protective clothing the medieval soldier carried a range of weapons. A double-edged sword and dagger would normally be slung from a *baldrick*, or belt and would be carried by knights and foot soldiers alike. Other edged weapons included the falchion, which was a single-edged sword like a large meat cleaver and a local speciality known as the Jedburgh stave. The *halberd*, *poleaxe* or *bill* became popular in the 15th century and was used to devastating effect at Flodden. It was not suitable for use from horseback but was a vicious tool for pulling men off horses. In addition to these were mauls and maces, which were little more than clubs.

Medieval War Engines

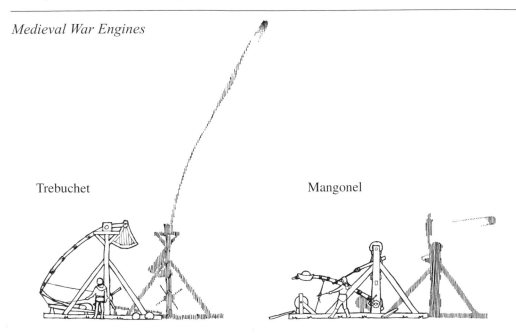

Trebuchet

Mangonel

Fig.11 The walls of castles were battered by stones or other kinds of missile hurled from large engines. The trebuchet employed a heavy weight to sling missiles high into the air, whence they crashed down almost vertically. The mangonel used torsion, like a large catapult, and fired at a low trajectory.

Spears were used but for stabbing rather than throwing. Mounted knights carried lances, to skewer their enemies but Wallace's soldiers countered these with long pikes, on which the knights' mighty horses were impaled.

Although there were archers on both sides, the English archers preferred a longer bow. Bow-butts beside Hume Castle, Bow Butts in the Old Town of Galashiels and The Butts in Kelso mark three of the ranges where archers practised in the later Middle Ages on the *butts* or targets. The crossbow was powerful, accurate and deadly, but slow to load and thus better suited to siege warfare. The rapid fire of the long bow, on the other hand, overcame its shortcomings, and its superiority on the battlefield was established in the defeat of King David II's French allies at Crécy in 1346.

Arrows played an important part in the victories of Falkirk and Halidon Hill but siege warfare required a much wider range of equipment. Some idea of the quantities of equipment used in King Edward I's campaigns can be gauged from receipts for material for the siege of Stirling Castle in 1304. One lists 6,050 crossbow bolts (short arrows) of 60cm (2ft) and 18,000 bolts of 30cm (1ft) as well as 336 goose wings, 360 feathers and wages for four men making arrows. Another lists 100 picks, mauls, 155 ameraxes (hammer-axes) for masons, six gavelocks (crowbars), 200 chisels, eighty coigns (wedges) and 100 trowels.

For the capture of Stirling, Edward I collected a siege train which included thirteen large engines. These included *trebuchets*, huge slings which used counter-balanced weights to fling stone balls high into the air, so that they struck vertically with the additional force which gravity provided **(fig.11)**.

Another engine used at this time was the *mangonel,* which hurled a missile at a much lower trajectory. Five years after the capture of Jedburgh an engine called "Esplante" was taken from there to the siege of Brechin (1303), but we are not told what kind of device this was.

Other large equipment consisted of battering rams, mantlets (movable wickerwork screens) and belfreys (raised fighting platforms).

War-making

Medieval nobles took their military role seriously. This is demonstrated in their official seals, which they used to endorse formal documents and on which they appear at full gallop, sword in hand and shield on arm. Such knights had conquered England in 1066 and in the 12th century, became an important feature of the new Scotland of King David I. Mounted, trained and well armoured, these soldiers were able to mount massed charges which neither dismounted men-at-arms, nor the untrained yokels of the feudal host were able to resist. Time and again the cavalry triumphed. It came as a shock, therefore, that the aristocratic knight found himself, not only resisted by common foot soldiers, but actually beaten by them.

Under normal conditions the foot soldier was no match for the armoured knight on horseback, unless he could keep him at a distance or stop his charging horse. Under William Wallace, Scottish soldiers found that horsemen could not penetrate a tight battle line of levelled spears. The *schiltron* formation used by Wallace at Stirling Bridge and by King Robert I at Bannockburn was highly successful in destroying the cohesion of mounted charges, while it also gave all-round protection to bodies of foot soldiers and enabled them to attack.

Longbowmen put the sting into the English armies of the 14th and 15th centuries. King Edward I had witnessed for himself the deadly effect of the long bow at the hands of the Welsh and used his new discovery to advantage at Falkirk, where his archers broke up Wallace's schiltrons. Although Selkirk archers fought against Edward at Falkirk, greater emphasis and constant practice was to give English bowmen a distinct advantage. Used against cavalry, the bow could cut down horses and men whose chain mail gave little protection against arrows. Under King Edward III at Halidon Hill the English learned to place archers forward of the battle line in "harrow" formation, where they could shoot to their sides as well as to their front. In the 15th century English archers also carried a sharpened stake, which they would drive into the ground to form a bristling barrier of *chevaux de frise,* and thereby keep horsemen at bay **(fig.12)**.

These tactics may have been employed in pitched battles but such occasions were rare, and were brought about as part of a wider strategy. English kings tried to use superior numbers to defeat the Scottish armies in pitched battles and to impose their will through garrisons in strongholds.

Scottish commanders, on the other hand, found that they could successfully frustrate this strategy by avoiding battle, so that their forces remained intact and by destroying any stronghold which fell to them, thereby denying

Medieval Battle Formations

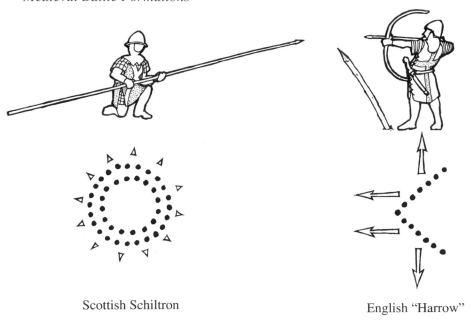

Scottish Schiltron	English "Harrow"

Fig.12 *In the late 13th and 14th centuries Scottish and English foot soldiers developed ways to defeat mounted knights. The circular schiltron formation could break up a cavalry charge, and archers in a "harrow" or wedge formation could attack horses and riders from a distance. When these formations met in battle the bowmen had a clear advantage over the spearmen.*

their future use to English garrisons. Even castles could become little better than prisons at times.

William Wallace in the Borders

Tweeddale and the Berwickshire coast featured largely in most of King Edward I's attempts to bring Scotland under his domination. His first campaign, in 1296, was on the surface a great success. His bloody capture of Berwick, which saw the townsmen put to death as punishment for their resistance, enabled him to advance to Dunbar, where he defeated King John's field army. By the end of the summer he had not only Edinburgh, Roxburgh and Jedburgh but the Scottish king himself.

It was at this low point for Scotland that William Wallace and Andrew Murray emerged to lead the resistance to Edward, as well as against some of their own countrymen. In 1297 Wallace's forces emerged from Selkirk Forest to attack the Bishop of Glasgow's house at Ancrum, before they went on later in the summer to defeat an English army at Stirling Bridge. After the battle they followed the English force almost to Berwick but refused to indulge in a second battle at Hutton Moor and instead retired to camp in Duns Park.

Wallace next launched an invasion of northern England and penetrated into Yorkshire before returning north. It was at this point that he was appointed "Guardian of the Realm", a ceremony which supposedly took place in the Kirk o' the Forest in Selkirk.

In 1298, as Wallace's force besieged Roxburgh Castle it was forced to retire when faced with the approach of a larger English army. Wallace retired to Falkirk, where his forces were soundly beaten in pitched battle by the army of the English king. Edward also captured Jedburgh in this campaign, whereupon Wallace resigned his appointment as Guardian and retired to Selkirk Forest to carry on his guerrilla war.

Although Wallace's men captured the new pele at Selkirk early in 1303, by the following winter, Edward's other garrisons at Lochmaben and Linlithgow still held onto his gains in southern Scotland. Furthermore, his armies had progressed beyond the Tay and were raiding from a base at Dunfermline. One such force caught Wallace, Simon Fraser and their men unawares at Happrew (Stobo) in Tweeddale. Although the two leaders escaped capture this time, Wallace was taken by his countrymen and given up to Edward in 1305.

Wallace's experience demonstrates how the opposing leaders waged war. The English king sought to destroy field armies in pitched battle (successfully at Dunbar and Falkirk) and control the country with garrisons. Wallace also desired to destroy the invaders and was fortunate to be able to carry the war into England after Stirling Bridge. Following his defeat at Falkirk, Wallace realised that his hope lay in guerrilla tactics waged from Selkirk Forest against isolated garrisons.

Had the forest extended further east and threatened communications with England, Wallace's presence could have been a serious obstacle to the English king. As it was, Edward was able to carry the war into central and north-east Scotland by land and sea. Wallace's methods were nevertheless appropriate for inferior numbers in forested hill country unsuited to cavalry and hit-and-run tactics coupled with the scale of Scotland's landmass combined, in the long run, to deter Edward's successors from their ambitions of conquest.

The impact which Wallace made on popular imagination is confirmed by places which bear his name, although in reality have no connection with him. Such is "Wallace's Trench" (Caddonfoot/ Yarrow), a much older earthwork on the Southern Upland Way between Traquair and Yair, "Wallace's Putting Stone" (Galashiels), and the 16th century "Wallace's Tower" (Roxburgh).

Sieges

The policy of English kings was to occupy castles and use them to dominate the surrounding countryside. King Robert I, on the other hand, destroyed strongholds which could be of value to the English. After a victory on the battlefield it was not unusual for castles to surrender to the winning side but sometimes a siege was necessary to win a castle.

To besiege a fortress all that was necessary was to surround it and prevent any opponent leaving or entering it. This made the garrison dependent upon whatever food or water they had with them, and starvation was the best way to ensure the capture of the strongest castles. Whenever possible, however, commanders preferred to capture a castle without unnecessary delay, as siege camps were places where disease could quickly spread. To achieve this end, psychology was also used,

Fig.13 Roxburgh Castle between the Rivers Teviot and Tweed was one of the strongest fortresses in Scotland, but was so close to the border that for much of its history it was in English hands. It was twice captured by stealth, by Sir James Douglas in 1313 and by Sir Alexander Ramsay in 1342. It was destroyed after the siege of 1460 but an artillery fort was constructed on the site in 1547.

with promises of better treatment of the defenders if they surrendered in an orderly manner rather than being taken by storm.

The pace of a siege was influenced not only by the demands of the campaign as a whole but also by the strength of the fortifications. In 1296 the town defences of Berwick were so weak that King Edward I's forces quickly carried them by storm, with some of the attackers actually riding over the defences on horseback. Although the castle defences were better, the garrison surrendered when they saw the town fall.

Where stronger resistance was encountered, a fortress might be subjected to battering by stone-hurling engines, or the walls could be weakened by *sapping* or *undermining*. The morale of the defenders could be further lowered by sniping crossbowmen and a siege tower was sometimes built to allow bowmen to see over the walls into a castle.

We know more about events at Roxburgh Castle than any other Borders stronghold. It occupied a strong position on high ground between the rivers Tweed and Teviot and had already been the subject of a fictional siege in the book, *'Roman de Fergus'* a century before its involvement in the Wars of Independence.

Edward I and his successors appointed only their most worthy leaders as Keepers of the castle, for their duties also included the administration of the county and town of Roxburgh. During Sir Robert Hastangs' appointment (1296-1305) he was supported by a garrison which varied in numbers from ten men-at-arms and 180 foot, to twenty men-at-arms and one hundred foot. Also kept at the castle was a carpenter, smith, mason, bowser (bowmaker) and watchman.

In spite of its present appearance, the castle was a large one in contrast to the single towers which became the norm in Scotland **(fig.13)**.

By the early 15th century the castle walls included several towers, one of which was a *donjon* or keep. Only on the west, where the ground is relatively level, could the castle be approached without a steep climb.

Roxburgh was a strong defence against conventional assault and withstood a siege by Wallace in 1297. Later events showed that where strength was not enough, ingenuity could succeed. The castle was captured in a night attack on 19 February 1313 while the garrison celebrated the feast of Shrove Tuesday. Sir James Douglas and his men approached the castle in the dark, dressed in black and on their hands and knees so that they would be mistaken for the small cattle of the time. Grappling hooks secured access to the wall-head by rope ladders and a sentry was silenced "with ane knyff". Although surprised, the garrison retired to the donjon, but their commander, William de Fiennes was wounded by an arrow and the tower was captured. Consistent with Robert's policy, the castle was burned. However, it was repaired and remained in Scottish hands for the next twenty-one years, after which King Edward granted the castle to Edward III.

At dawn on 30 March 1342 the castle fell in another surprise *escalade*, this time to a force led by Alexander Ramsay. Afterwards he enjoyed a short career as Warden and Sheriff of Teviotdale until he was starved to death in Hermitage Castle by Sir William Douglas, "Knight of Liddesdale".

After the battle of Neville's Cross Roxburgh returned to English hands and it remained so for more than a century. In August 1436 King James I besieged the castle and town without success for a fortnight. Moreover, divisions in his army and the approach of an English force obliged him to leave behind all the expensive siege artillery which he had prepared or had imported from Flanders.

Roxburgh's final destruction came in 1460 when it was successfully stormed after being bombarded with cannon under the close direction of the king himself. King James II took a keen interest in the new artillery and took "plesure in dischargeng gret gunis", one of which burst and killed him. Thus was fulfilled an old prophecy which told that Roxburgh would only fall to a dead man. The castle was then destroyed and not rebuilt.

The final siege of Roxburgh marks a significant stage in medieval warfare, for this castle which had withstood conventional attack, and humiliated James I a generation earlier, was taken only with the aid of cannon, which it was not designed to resist. A new era of warfare was approaching which would come to be dominated by gunpowder and which would last until modern times.

Warfare in the age of gunpowder

The development of guns

Use of gunpowder in Britain may have originated in the experiments of the 13th century English friar, Roger Bacon, although it had been known in China for at least two centuries before that. Gunpowder is known to have been manufactured in England in the 1330s and the English may have used guns at Crécy. In 1384 a man called Dietrich, who worked at Edinburgh Castle, provided a device called a "gun" for £4, and materials for the manufacture of gunpowder were sent to various castles in Scotland.

An early cannon is shown in an English manuscript of 1326 and English royal accounts show that the walls of Berwick were stocked with guns in 1384. These references show that from its early development gunpowder was used for artillery, which would be served by a team of gunners and for firearms carried by individual soldiers. Illuminated manuscripts of 15th century wars show both types in use and during this period the bowman lost his command of the battlefield as guns became more widely used.

Early cannon were little more than tubes made of wrought iron strips reinforced with iron hoops (hence the name "barrel") or cast from brass in much the same way as church bells. They were fastened to wooden frames without wheels, with nothing to absorb the recoil when the gun fired. In 1442 Mr Nicolas, a carpenter was sent to "Galowayscheelis" (Galashiels) regarding the carriage of the King's great bombard, though whether it was to attend the gun itself, or to obtain timber for its repair, is not clear. In the 15th century the first wheeled carriages were provided, along with barrels which could be adjusted for range by elevating or lowering the muzzle (mouth). This added mobility made cannon more useful on the battlefield and by the time of Flodden, artillery had become an important part of a field army **(fig.14)**.

Hand guns were at first small tubes fastened to the front of long handles, set off by a light at a simple touch hole. A hook beneath the gun helped to prevent the gun recoiling when fired from a castle window or protective cover.

Early Artillery

15th century bombard "Mons Meg"

15th/ 16th century breech loader

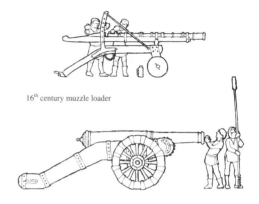

16th century muzzle loader

Fig.14 Gunpowder fired stones at castle walls with much greater force than mangonels or trebuchets, and great guns like Mons Meg were built to smash masonry. Smaller, more mobile guns could also be used on the battlefield. Breech loading and muzzle loading guns were used at Eyemouth Fort, but the latter came to dominate the battlefield until more effective breech loading guns were developed in the 19th century.

In the 15th century a mechanical *lock* was added to assist firing by pressing a smouldering cord (a "match") onto the exposed touch hole. This was improved in turn, by the wheel lock and the flint lock which operated much like a cigarette lighter and reduced the danger of accidental discharge. Longer barrels gave greater range, so that by the early 16th century the hand gun had become the musket, the first recognisable ancestor of the modern rifle. As there was also a call for short barrelled guns, a separate class of firearm developed, the pistol.

16th Century Arms and Armour

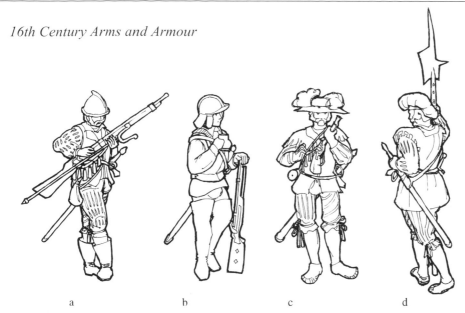

a   b   c   d

Fig.15 Soldiers of the Rough Wooing of the 1540s: (a) soldier armed with a matchlock musket (hackbutt), bandolier, sword and helmet; (b) a Border light horseman in steel back-and breast and "lobster" helmet with sword and hackbutt; (c) German mercenary with sword and wheel-lock pistol; (d) billman with sword and halberd (billhook).

Cannon, muskets and pistols continued to be developed and improved, particularly in matters of range, accuracy and rate of fire. It needed an Industrial Revolution, however, to produce the rifled barrels of two Victorian guns which are mounted on Fort Point (Eyemouth). It took brass cartridges to enable James Paris Lee of Hawick to design the loading action on which the Lee Enfield (the standard rifle of the British Army in both World Wars) was based.

Equipment and dress

Although cannon and firearms were new weapons, much of the basic armoury of the soldier continued along traditional lines until the later 17th century. The sword retained its importance for close quarter fighting into the 19th century, although latterly it was carried only by officers **(fig.15)**.

On the other hand, the 16th century Muster Rolls for the Borders indicate that the most common weapon was the spear, whereas swords are not mentioned as often as might be expected. Some well-made swords survive from this period, with German blades and barred protection for the knuckles. Basket hilted broadswords predominated among the less wealthy near the end of the 16th century, while the nobility wore rapiers and parrying daggers. Dirks, home-made fighting knives and long narrow daggers appear to have been carried by all and sundry, including the clergy.

Horsemen continued to rely on the lance or *"lang spear"* combined with the weight of their horses but the large shield went out of use. The pike provided infantrymen with protection against cavalry until after the Civil Wars of the 1640s. It was replaced by the bayonet, a dagger which could be attached to the muzzle of a musket and thereby enable the infantryman to combine the roles of pikeman and musketeer.

While a knight in full armour was almost invulnerable to pointed or edged weapons, the impact of a gunstone or soft lead bullet could break an armour plate. A pair of cavalry breastplates with gunshot holes in them, brought back as souvenirs by Sir Walter Scott from the field of Waterloo, show this vulnerability only too well. They are now on display at Scott's home, Abbotsford (Melrose).

Thus, as the use of guns increased, armour was thickened to withstand the impact of bullets. As this also had the effect of greatly increasing its weight and manoeuvrability, full plate was used in the main for protection of the head, back and chest. By the 16th century many soldiers relied on toughened clothes rather than metal plate.

The brigandine or *jack* combined layers of quilted cloth with small overlapping plates of metal or horn, and extended from the neck to upper thigh. Additional protection could be provided by thigh length boots, reinforced gauntlets, chains of brass or pewter drawn four or five times along the thighs and sleeves and a scarf wrapped two or three times about the neck. This combination provided mobility and effective protection against edged weapons but would not stop a bullet.

The "Riding families" of Scotts, Kers (or Kerrs), Elliots, Turnbulls and others went about their illegal business of reiving in "steill bonnetts" (helmets) with breastplates or jacks and carried bucklers. Their dress was notably plainer in appearance than the soldiers who fought in the national armies of the day. Excellent representations of these light horsemen can be seen on statues in Selkirk (dismounted), Galashiels and Hawick.

The range of weapons and military dress as used by amateur soldiers is suggested by a muster which was taken at Peebles in 1572. A total of 161 men provided between them: one buckler, one *hackbutt,* two "guns", two axes, three lances, six forks, seven bows, thirty-three "bonnets", forty-three swords, fifty-four staves, sixty-five spears and, rather enigmatically, one bag. In addition, thirty-three men were described as "armit", which may indicate that they possessed jacks or other stout wear.

Professional soldiers often used their clothing to express their individuality. Many were 'dandies', and the Scottish, English, French, Spanish and Imperial armies which took part in the Border wars of the mid-16th century would have provided an abundance of colour in their dress.

The red uniform of the *'New Model Army'* in the 1640s was to dictate the colour worn by British infantry for the next 250 years. Leslie's Regiment, which became the King's Own Scottish Borderers, wore red coats until the late 19th century when they were replaced by khaki tunics, the forerunner of today's camouflage uniform. The return of the steel helmet for trench warfare during the First World War (a French innovation in late 1914) explains the appearance of the soldier depicted on the war memorials at Walkerburn (Innerleithen) and Minto.

War-making

In the renewed hostilities of the 16th century, cannon and firearms played an important part. When confident of victory, both sides preferred pitched battles and avoided time-consuming sieges, even though few fortresses were capable of withstanding the battering of cannon.

The first great battle should have been won by King James IV who, like his predecessors, took a strong interest in artillery and had amassed an impressive train of guns. At Flodden, however, the heavy artillery pieces used by the Scots achieved little, whereas the lighter English artillery provoked the Scots into the attack. Their king could not hold them back and giving up the advantage of the higher ground, he charged with them. The end result was a disastrous defeat for the Scots in which James and two dozen barons and earls were killed.

The battle was the climax of a major invasion of England which was designed to draw the English to battle and defeat. This was a similar tactic to that used by King Edward I in his invasions of Scotland two centuries earlier. During the first half of the 16th century, the Merse and Teviotdale saw several incursions by English armies, most of which were intended to bring on battle but without success. On the other hand, such raids maintained a constant pressure on the inhabitants and a number of Borders families served the English king at one time or other.

When they were not out thieving, reivers on both sides of the border formed the "prickers" or light horsemen in time of war. However, living on the Border and with friends as well as foes on the opposite side, they often confused self-interest with national needs. At Flodden, according to the Bishop of Durham, the English Borderers were "falser than Scots, and …when the battles joined …fell to rifling and robbing as well on our side as of the Scots …so that our folks as much fear the falsehood of them as they do the Scots". In 1545 the Earl of Hertford had to send Irishmen to ravage the valleys of the Kale and Bowmont because the "Borderers will not most willingly burn their neighbours".

A strategy of provocation was pursued at times by March Wardens and their captains in order to draw their opponents to a battle. In so doing they were repeating, with smaller forces at their disposal, the strategies of Edward I before Falkirk and James IV before Flodden. To the Border horsemen these raids were second nature and alliances were chosen carefully. In 1542 the Earl of Angus (a Douglas and a Scot) and his kinsmen joined with Robert Bowes (Warden of the English East March) in a raid into Teviotdale with 3,000 riders. They set an ambush for the Earl of Huntly on Hadden Rigg (Sprouston) but this turned into disaster when the Redesdale and Tynedale riders fled with their stolen cattle and the rest of the English followed suit.

An even more serious defeat followed in 1545, when an English force under Ralph Eure and Brian Laiton, retiring from Melrose laden with booty, was caught unawares on Lilliardsedge by the same Earl of Angus who had earlier been their ally **(fig.16)**. At the Battle of Ancrum Moor Eure's Scottish allies, drawn from the Teviotdale families of Croser and Nixon, tore off their English badges and joined

Fig.16 *The battlefield of Ancrum Moor from Lilliardsedge, looking towards the Eildon Hills.*

their countrymen in the attack. Eure and Laiton were killed and the battle did much to revive Scottish national pride after the disaster at Solway Moss.

Accounts of these battles suggest that most of the soldiers were mounted and that gunpowder played little part. Both English defeats provoked a stern response from King Henry VIII, who dispatched armies to ravage the lower Tweed and Teviotdale **(Plate 2)**. After Ancrum Moor the Earl of Hertford was sent north to inflict the worst damage of the war.

The Earl of Hertford's Invasion of 1545

During the summer rumours reached London, from Scots in English pay, of 200 gunners, 500 horse and 500 footmen sent from France to assist the Scots. King Henry VIII levied a royal army of 12,000 men "for the annoyance

of the Scots and Frenchmen intending displeasure to those parts". Most of these were raised in the north of England, but there was also a contingent from Ireland and alliance with Charles V (King of Spain and Holy Roman Emperor) brought mercenaries from Spain, the Netherlands, Germany, Italy and the Balkans. On the eve of the invasion, French officers crossed the Tweed to Wark Castle, where they offered their services to the English commander.

Henry's instructions to Hertford included fortification of Kelso Abbey, capture of Hume Castle, and devastation of the Borders countryside. This meant that by leaving garrisons at Hume, Kelso, Wark and Norham the English would be able to dominate Teviotdale and the Merse **(Plate 1)**.

The stout walls of Kelso Abbey church **(Plate 8)** provided a first line of defence for the Scots

Attack on Jedburgh 1545

Fig.17 *In September 1545 the Earl of Hertford's soldiers burned Jedburgh, including the town, the Augustinian abbey and the Franciscan friary.*

and a force of one hundred men with twelve monks was inside. After the York Herald had called on the garrison to surrender without success, English cannon made a breach in the walls. Signor de Gamboa's Spaniards led the first assault in which three or four were shot by Scottish hackbutters (musketeers) but succeeded in driving the defenders into the tower.

During the night, thirteen of the defenders escaped over the wall, possibly with the help of bell ropes, but two were captured and killed. By morning, the Spaniards had won the tower and killed the remaining garrison. Hertford examined the abbey with his engineers but rejected it as the site for a future fortress in favour of the ruins of Roxburgh Castle.

Over the next few days Hertford's horsemen raided Tweeddale as far as Dryburgh and Melrose, both of which abbeys they burnt but they needed the assistance of two cannon to secure the capture of Dalcove Tower (Mertoun). The Spaniards dismantled Kelso Abbey and sent the lead from its roof in wagons to Wark Castle.

The Earl of Angus had to content himself with annoying Hertford's army as best he could with his "prickers" and some running fights took place between the light cavalry of both sides. Gavin Hume narrowly escaped capture by taking refuge in Hume Castle, which was one objective Hertford failed to take that year.

From Kelso the English army marched up Teviotdale, burning homes and the newly gathered corn as they went. Two bronze bells (one of which is now in the Museum of Scotland) may have come from Kelso Abbey and been left on the English camp site at Roxburgh Mains where they were turned up during ploughing.

From there, Robert Bowes with 1,500 light horse, burnt the villages of Teviotdale as far west as Denholm (Hawick), Minto and the Rule Water. Hertford, with the remaining horse, some footmen, the Irish contingent and one hundred hackbutters burnt the Abbey, Friary and town of Jedburgh **(fig.17)**. He also sacked all dwellings for two miles around, with the exception of the homes of the Kerrs who pleaded their loyalty to the English king.

Fourteen or fifteen settlements in the Kale and Bowmont valleys were burned before the English force re-crossed the border to Wark. Meanwhile, the Scots had retaliated by burning Horncliff (Northumberland), but were repulsed by horsemen from garrisons based on the English side of the Tweed.

From Wark the horsemen devastated the countryside as far as Hume, where they devastated everything up to the castle walls, and went on to destroy Eccles and Coldstream nunneries, the town of Duns and the surrounding villages, before returning to the Tweed where the army stood down.

Hertford's soldiers ravaged Teviotdale, much of Tweeddale and the Merse. However, they still failed to bring the Earl of Angus' army to a pitched battle, and at the end of the day abandoned the ground which they had occupied.

Garrisons

For the first time since the Wars of Independence, foreign garrisons were systematically installed on Scottish soil as a result of renewed hostility between the two neighbouring countries. Although many of these were English, some were troops provided by France, not only to reinforce Scottish opposition to England, but also to strengthen French influence over Scotland. Because of the impact which gunpowder had made upon traditional defences, these garrisons were installed, where possible, in defences which incorporated the latest designs to resist cannon balls.

Hertford's capture of Kelso Abbey, and his dispatch of two guns to Dalcove Tower show how quickly cannon, or even the threat of their use, could bring about the surrender of buildings which in earlier times would have held out for much longer.

Gun-loops became a common defensive feature in the course of the 16th century **(fig.18)** and can be seen in the towers of Greenknowe (Gordon) and Drumlanrig, the Commendator's Houses of Melrose and Dryburgh Abbeys, and in the surviving corner tower of Peebles Town Wall. These were mostly intended for the use of defenders armed with hackbutts or hand guns, although grander fortresses such as Hermitage might also have deployed cannon.

The defenders in these places were able to carry out an active defence of sorts, as Spanish soldiers killed in the attack on Kelso Abbey bear witness, but square stone buildings failed to provide an all-round field of fire, and were vulnerable to attackers' cannon. One tower

Loopholes

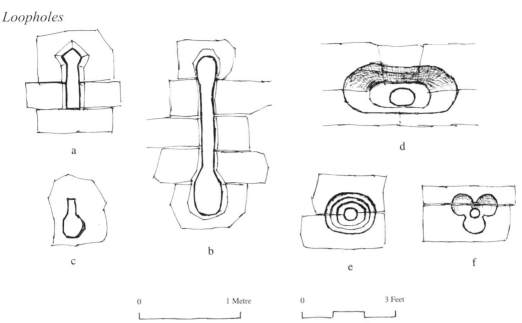

a

b

c

d

e

f

0   1 Metre   0   3 Feet

Fig.18 *Loophole types from Border castles: (a) Neidpath: arrow loop, 14th century. (b) Hume: gun loop, late 14th/ early 15th century; (c) Newark: gun loop, late 15th century; (d) Hermitage: gun loop, mid-16th century; (e, f) Drochil: shot holes, late 16th century.*

where the field of fire was improved by design was Littledean (Maxton: **fig.19**). Remodelled from a square plan, one side of this tower consisted of a semi-circular front pierced close to the ground by gun-loops. These were close enough together for their fields of fire to overlap, and were low enough for their horizontal fire to *rake* the approaches, so that if a shot missed one attacker it had a good chance of hitting somebody further away.

These features helped traditional stone castles and towers to put up a spirited resistance, but stone walls were vulnerable to cannon fire, at a time when guns were increasing in numbers and use. On the Anglo-Scottish border in the early 16th century military engineers had ample opportunities to apply lessons learned elsewhere, especially in Italy, where wealthy warring states had made considerable progress in alternative ways to counter gunfire.

In 1544 King Henry VIII was planning the establishment of garrisons on both sides of the border to neutralise any opposition in the Merse and Teviotdale. In November he sent an Italian engineer called Antonio Arcani to advise on the defensive possibilities of Coldingham Priory, and the following year the Italian looked at Kelso Abbey. Although alternative sites at Eyemouth and Roxburgh Castle were eventually chosen because they offered greater scope for fortification, this was not necessarily because the churches were incapable of defence. Kelso may have been captured with relative ease by Hertford, but in 1544 George Bowes with a small force had held Coldingham against the Earl of Arran and 8,000 men. In 1548 Jedburgh Abbey was turned into a fortress by the French General D'Essé to defend the town against the English.

Fig.19 *Littledean Tower beside the River Tweed. The semi-circular front, which recalls towers in the royal palaces of Falkland and Holyrood, not only increased the field of fire, but also added to the owner's prestige.*

Although it was easier and cheaper to adapt existing buildings to artillery defences, if they proved ineffective, the exercise represented false economy. On the English bank of the Tweed, artillery towers were added to Norham Castle. At Berwick the massive Lord's Mount tower was added to the medieval walls and the Norman motte of Wark Castle was converted to an artillery defence during this period. At Roxburgh a new fort was constructed within the ruins of the former castle which occupied a strong position of great strategic importance. Some of the earlier ruins were incorporated into the design, which made use of thick, low ramparts of earth behind dry ditches. The fort was broadly rectangular in plan and in three places guns were installed to fire along the face of the

rampart, that is, *enfilade* (take in cross-fire) any attackers who might gather there and so wreak the greatest havoc.

The principles of flanking fire had been adopted into castle building in the 13th century, when towers were added to the front of the curtain wall and loopholed in the sides for archers. Now the *bastion* replaced the flanking tower. It was no higher than the rampart but its two flanks held guns to sweep the front of the rampart and its front was pointed to eliminate "dead ground" where an attacker might be safe from flanking fire **(fig.20)**.

English garrisons were established between 1547-48 in artillery forts at Roxburgh, Eyemouth **(Plate 9)** and Lauder and plans of all three forts have survived. Hume was also garrisoned following its surrender after Pinkie, although there is no indication that the existing castle was altered. Roxburgh and Eyemouth were new bastion forts designed by Sir Richard Lee, who had experience of such work in the English oversees territories around Calais and who was later to design the walls of Berwick upon Tweed.

At Eyemouth, Lee fortified the headland which dominates the harbour and town. His fort cost £1,908 to build and £3,598 to run between September 1548 and August 1550. The garrison consisted of a captain, a number of lieutenants, a master gunner, two porters, a drummer, a surgeon, an ensign, a clerk, ten light horsemen and thirty-four hackbutters. The armament consisted of six guns: a *saker*, a *falcon* and four *fowlers*, to which were later added four more pieces (a fowler, a *falconet* and two *demi-culverins*). Because of its position, Eyemouth fort provided a base from

Fig.20 The 16th century walls of Berwick upon Tweed illustrate principles of defence in artillery forts. Guns placed in the flanks of a bastion could cover the face of the neighbouring bastion and catch any attacking force in cross-fire.

Frenchman who was appointed Principal Master Mason to Mary, Queen of Scots in 1557. The French fort was stronger and occupied a larger area than the English fort of a decade earlier. In 1559 the fort was able to lend twelve large guns for the intended siege of Wark Castle and send 200 men to Kinghorn in Fife. Not only did this fort duplicate the functions of the earlier English work, but it provided a sufficient menace to Berwick upon Tweed for the English crown to embark upon a long and expensive programme of refortification **(Plate 10)**.

Following the evacuation and slighting of the French fortifications by the Treaty of Cateau Cambrèsis in 1559, no garrison forts remained in the Borders. Not until the troubles of the mid-17th century were strongholds once again garrisoned for war. In the Borders, Coldingham Priory and Neidpath Castle (Peebles) would have stood little chance against the guns of Oliver Cromwell and General Lambert. The occupation of Scotland by the New Model Army, the first national standing army and precursor to the British Army, was more effectively achieved than any attempt by King Edward I or his descendants. Throughout the 1650s, troops were billeted in Borders households, who were responsible for their upkeep. Hence records tell of requirements "to send hay or straw to Selkirk for 80 horse … for captayne Lloyd's troop" in 1651 and of quartering Twistleton's regiment at Peebles the following year. It was from the frontier town of Coldstream in 1660 that General Monck led his regiment, later to become the Coldstream Guards, in support of the Restoration of King Charles II.

which to dominate the countryside and a staging post on the route between Berwick and English forts in Lothian. Thomas Gower, an accomplished engineer and the first captain, complained that in addition to ruling the country and dealing with military passengers, he was also commanded to leave his post whenever the king had need of his services elsewhere.

Although the English forts in the Borders were evacuated and demolished in 1550, French ambitions in Scotland included a building programme and the establishment of garrisons in the years 1555-1557. These included the construction of a new fort at Eyemouth, possibly at the hands of "Johnne Roytell", the

Sieges

King James II used guns to subdue the powerful Douglas family in the mid-15th century before his ill-fated use of them at Roxburgh. Although the manner of the king's death reveals an important weakness of early artillery, the successful storming of Roxburgh at the conclusion of the siege is an indication that its walls, which had withstood the engines of King James I in 1434, were not able to resist the improved artillery of his son.

Heavy guns were most commonly used to batter the walls of fortresses and their lack of manoeuvrability made them unsuitable for battlefield campaigning. The great gun, Mons Meg took almost two weeks to travel the fifty miles from Edinburgh to the siege of Norham Castle in 1497. Although cast metal balls only gradually replaced stone balls, the effect of gunfire on castle walls was far greater than earlier stone-throwing engines. Narrow stone walls built for height tended to shatter under bombardment, so defending engineers took steps to counter these effects by building lower walls and piling earth behind to absorb the shock of the cannon balls.

The courtyard wall of Cessford Castle was improved in this way and in 1523 was described by an English assailant as "vawmewred (fore-walled) with earth of the best sort that I have seen". The English guns made little impression on this wall although they opened up a blocked window in the main tower. This gave access to a chamber which the gunners attempted to pack with gunpowder, but their attempt to mine the building was foiled. The castle did not succumb to storm but was surrendered by the owner, Sir Andrew Ker, who had been elsewhere when the siege began.

Gunpowder altered the scale of the killing zone between opposing forces, by greatly extending the range of lethal missiles, whether bullets, *grape shot* or cannon balls. Although the custom-built artillery defences of Haddington and Leith in Lothian were subjected to prolonged sieges, the forts at Lauder, Roxburgh and Eyemouth were never put to the test. Had they been attacked, they would have proved far more deadly to a storming party than any medieval defences.

The work of gunners at Kelso Abbey in 1545, Hume Castle in 1569, Coldingham Priory in 1650 showed that even thick stone walls would not resist continual pounding from guns. Not surprisingly, defenders of traditional towers and castles felt less and less inclined to trust in stone walls as a protection against cannon fire, and the mere presence of artillery was sometimes enough to bring about the surrender of a tower.

The relationship of Scotland and England after 1603, and particularly after 1707, was quite different from that which existed between continental powers, which continued to fortify their frontier regions into modern times. Berwick upon Tweed was besieged during the Civil War, but the power of gunpowder had made prolonged resistance in unsuitable defences a thing of the past.

Warfare in the Industrial Age

The British Army grew out of a small number of regiments which were raised by parliament during the Civil War, augmented by additional troops raised to protect King Charles II and his overseas possessions. The Borders has provided recruits for many branches of the armed services but has a particular connection with the King's Own Scottish Borderers (KOSB). At various times a *militia* of part-time soldiers was raised to defend the Borders from attack but despite one embarrassing false alarm during the Napoleonic Wars, when the warning beacon at Hume Castle was lit in error, the occasion for their use did not arise.

The KOSB defended the national interest against insurrection and foreign enemies. It played an active part in the suppression of Jacobite risings, and fought with distinction in many conflicts abroad. The regiment was increased in size, when necessary, to reflect the needs of overseas empire and the dangers of European and world wars and in 1916 compulsory conscription replaced voluntary enlistment for the first time.

The wide open spaces of the Borders provided a valuable training ground for all units of the British Army and Stobs Camp, established in 1903, could hold up to 100,000 men at one time.

The Industrial Revolution greatly increased the sophistication and variety of weapons and in World War I the KOSB faced high explosive shells, poison gas and machine guns on the nightmare battlefields of the Western Front and at Gallipoli. As the Borders was now within reach of enemy *zeppelins* and warships, some protection was provided by 77 Squadron, Royal Flying Corps (later Royal Air Force) based at Charterhall, Whinfield and Whiteburn (Westruther) and by guns emplaced on Fort Point. At the same time, civilians began to take a much more active part in the war effort.

The defeat of the British Expeditionary Force and allied forces, and their withdrawal from Dunkirk in 1940 led to the re-organisation of home defences. The Local Defence Volunteers (later Home Guard) revived the spirit of the earlier militia and carried out various well-meaning, but strategically limited anti-invasion works. These included loopholes on the old bridge at Ancrum and in the Haining gate (Selkirk) and a pill box and loopholes to cover Kelso bridge and the river downstream from it.

In 1942 the RAF re-occupied the two main Berwickshire airfields. Charterhall was the base, with Whinfield as its satellite station and both were occupied by 54 OTU (Operational Training Unit). In January 1945 a total of eighty-eight bombers and fighter-bombers were stationed at Charterhall.

Although the region attracted little attention from enemy aircraft, and air raid shelters in Borders' towns were not needed, the region did contain a vitally important munitions factory at Charlesfield, where Imperial Chemical Industries (ICI) Ltd. opened an extensive plant in 1943. This was one of only two factories in Britain which produced incendiary bombs in large numbers for the Strategic Bombing Campaign, and by May 1945 nearly twenty-four million bombs had been assembled there **(fig.21)**.

Fig.21 *The large Charlesfield munitions factory produced millions of stick-like incendiary bombs in World War II. Most of the work was carried out by women, as men were needed for military service.*

War memorials in every town and village record the names of Borderers who lost their lives in the armed services during both World Wars. A memorial to the Free Polish forces in Duns is just one poignant reminder that the Borders provided a home to soldiers of other nations in the Second World War.

Not all of the servicemen who visited the Borders during the wars did so voluntarily. There were Prisoner of War Camps in the Borders at Dawyck (Drumelzier), Annay Road (Melrose), Newtown St Boswells and Stobs Camp. These were temporary wood-built structures that, in the case of Dawyck, housed on average one hundred POW's during the First World War. When they were dismantled they left little or no trace and the exact location of those mentioned above cannot be easily identified.

Although the arrival of the nuclear age rendered all former fortification systems obsolete, it did not, unhappily, remove the need for defence systems. In the coastal area the Cold War saw the installation of early warning posts and secret bunkers, such as one at Crosslaw (Coldingham), as well as the emergency control centre in Scottish Borders Council headquarters. Conscription was continued after 1945 in the form of National Service and many Borderers served in overseas dominions, which grew fewer as independence spread. Many national servicemen passed through the army camp at Stobs, which continued to provide accommodation up to its closure in 1959.

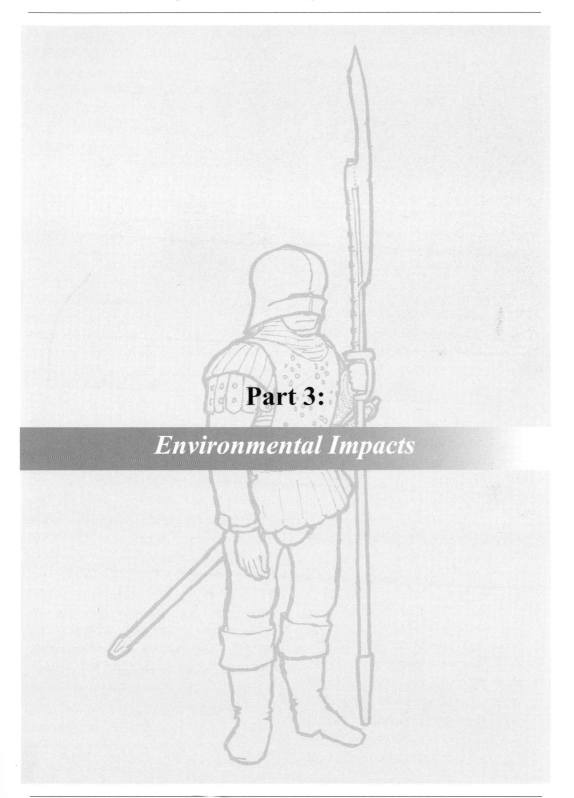

Part 3:

Environmental Impacts

Part 3: Environmental Impacts

The Scottish Borders are part of a frontier zone which for much of history separated two hostile nations. For this reason the people held themselves ready for war even in times of peace and landowners who made up the wartime leaders not only trained for war in the chase but prepared their defences accordingly. The advent of war proper put these preparations to the test and affected not only the people but also the environment of the Borders.

Training for war

An idealised code of conduct evolved amongst the aristocracy by which the medieval knight was expected to perform chivalrous deeds from horseback. To do this he learnt to ride from childhood and hunted down wild animals with spear or lance, in the same way in which he would ride down an enemy's foot soldiers. Constant practice was required to achieve and maintain the required level of skill and this was found in hunting. While the gentry practised on horseback, their tenants acquired skills on foot with spear and bow and arrow, skills which would be put to the test at Falkirk where Wallace's archers were drawn from Selkirk Forest. A statute of King James I, who had seen English archers at work in France, ordered that butts were to be set up near churches for archery practice on holy days.

In order to conserve countryside over which to hunt and conserve game for the chase, hunting forests were identified in law and the range of activities within them strictly controlled by sheriffs and foresters. Unauthorised hunting in these forests warranted a ten pound fine (a cow cost 46 pence, a sheep 7 pence in 1328) and there were restrictions on collection of wood for fuel, timber for building and the pasturing of livestock. King David I established forests based on the Anglo-Norman model of royal hunting reserves and the earliest of these is recorded in his charter to Melrose Abbey, issued around 1136. This gave the monks rights to cut timber and keep pigs ("pannage") in the forests of Selkirk and Traquair. Several years afterwards we hear of other forests based upon the Gala and Leader Waters. The forest of Selkirk, Ettrick and Traquair (better known simply as Ettrick Forest) and Jedforest were the longest lived of these royal reserves. The Capon Tree (Jedburgh: **fig.22**) which stands besides the A68 just south of Jedburgh, is one of a few ancient trees which survive from the latter.

The management of forests depended greatly on the interests of the monarch of the time. Although all the kings appear to have had at least a passing interest in hunting as a pursuit, the degree with which they looked after their assets varied. King James II in particular, took an active interest in the administration of the hunting reserves and expanded or acquired many royal reserves. Having the status of a royal forest did not provide a forest with complete protection from deforestation. On occasion woodland was actively felled as was the case in the forest of Gala and Leader during the reign of King Alexander II. Encroachment on royal forests for cultivation ("assarts") was granted under special licence and in the long term was responsible for the disappearance of the woodland. King Charles I imposed fines on landowners who had encroached on the forest without licence and this was one source

1. Hume Castle is the chief fortress of the Merse, a deceptively tame-looking landscape of cultivated fields ...h has, nevertheless, seen the passage of many armies.

2. Teviotdale seen from Peniel Heugh, Ancrum. Flanked by rugged volcanic hills, this valley was devastated ...merous occasions and housed many of the most active Border reivers.

Plate 3. Hawick Motte, the earthwork remains of a Norman castle.

Plate 4. Neidpath Castle, chief stronghold of Tweeddale in the 14th century, dominates the River Tweed as it v
through Neidpath Gorge.

e 5. Cessford Castle, built in the 15th century, was besieged by the Earl of Surrey in 1523.

e 6. Smailholm Tower is a landmark for miles around and still retains its barmkin wall.

Plate 7. Greenknowe Tower is a fine "L-plan" tower of the later 16th century.

Plate 8. Kelso Abbey was sacked after a dramatic attack by Spanish troops in 1545.

9. Eyemouth artillery fort incorporated new methods of fortress design. An earlier, English defence was ~porated ten years later into a larger fort built by Scotland's French allies in 1557 (see reconstruction, **Fig.33**).

10. Berwick upon Tweed changed hands several times and is now part of England. Construction of a French nearby Eyemouth (**Plate 9**) provoked the complete redesign of the town defences to accommodate artillery in d bastions (see **Fig.27**).

Plate 11. Hume Castle sits on a volcanic crag and was turned into a folly, landmark and viewpoint in the century. Even so, its walls still contain medieval masonry.

Plate 12. Mary Queen of Scots House is one of several fortified houses which once existed in Jedburgh. present form it incorporates a 16th century bastle house with a 17th century wing and stair turret.

e 13. Kilnsike Tower is a fortified farmhouse (bastle or pele house), entry to which was by a wooden stair to a at first floor level. A door in the gable led to a basement, which could accommodate animals in time of danger.

14. Peebles Town Wall was built between 1570 and 1574, but on a much smaller scale than the English walls rwick (see **Plate 10**). The wall was approximately four metres high with "blockhouses" at convenient points. uch blockhouse, with two gun ports and the adjoining stretches of wall, still survives.

Plate 15. The Covenanters' Redoubt on Duns Law is a rare example of a military fieldwork. It dates from the Bishop's War of 1639, when General Leslie's forces assembled on the hill in defiance of King Charles I.

Plate 16. Drumlanrig's Tower, Hawick was built in the 16th century tower and extended and converted i[nto] luxurious town house by the Duchess of Buccleuch in the late 17th century. The building now contains an interpret[ive] centre with a vivid account of the reiving era.

Fig.22 *The Capon Tree near Jedburgh is a centuries old survivor of the medieval Jedforest.*

of friction in the years before the Civil War.

Artificial chases could be created as parks for the confinement and hunting of deer. The park of Jedburgh was formed from part of the older Jedforest. Such parks were enclosed by an earthen bank and internal ditch usually surmounted by a fence, *palisade* or wall, structures known as the "park pale". These parks often adjoined the castle or residence of the landowner and many were recorded by the 16th century map maker, Timothy Pont. Royal parks were administered by a keeper, who was normally drawn from a prominent local land owning family. For example in 1452, Thomas Home was appointed hereditary keeper of the royal park at Duns where Wallace's force had camped after Stirling Bridge. The White Dyke, visible on the hillside around Hermitage

Castle, may be the remains of such a pale. Another at the Haining, originally linked with the royal castle of Selkirk, may have continued in use after the castle's destruction early in the 14th century.

As a result of hunting, the medieval period saw the extinction of some of the larger native species. Wild boar and red deer were favourite targets for hunting expeditions and also provided a good source of meat and skins. The boar may have survived into the 12th century but was probably hunted out soon after. The red deer survived longer than this, but it was also hunted to extinction in south eastern Scotland during the Middle Ages.

The wolf was seen as a dangerous predator and may well have been a threat to the

Fig.23 *World War I practice trenches still survive on the moors near the site of Stobs Camp, and can be identified from the zigzag or "castle wall" course which they followed to minimise the blast effect of exploding shells.*

increasingly large flocks of sheep which were kept on the Border hills. The wolf was such a problem that, in the 15th century parliament passed several Acts encouraging wolf hunting. The importance placed upon this is illustrated by an Act of 1457-8 which put a bounty of one Scots penny per wolf, to be paid from every householder in the parish in which the beast was killed. Shortly after the bailie of the earldom of March paid Gilbert Home five shillings for killing ten wolves in Cockburnspath. As a result of these acts the wolf became the target of huntsmen and was wiped out in the Borders along with the boar and red deer. Similarly, the beaver had no value as a food source but had been hunted to extinction for its pelt by the 16th century.

The popularity of fox hunting among soldiers in later years may explain why officials in Borders' hunts today dress in red ("pink")

which was the colour of the British Army tunic in the later 17th, 18th and 19th centuries.

In the present century, many parts of the Borders were used to train soldiers for service overseas, particularly around the extensive training camp at Stobs, where World War I trenches can still be detected in the moorland, along with tank tracks from World War II **(fig.23)**. The Eildon Hills include remains of two former firing ranges used by the Territorial Army and the Twinlaw Cairns (Westruther) on the Southern Upland Way had to be rebuilt after being damaged by tanks of the Free Polish Army.

Building for war

Many castles, towers and bastle houses still bear witness to the care with which landowners defended their homes. Earthwork defences were constructed by shaping the very ground on which they stood, as at Hawick Motte, Roxburgh Castle and Eyemouth Fort. Stone and timber, if not available on the spot, would have been brought from the nearest available sources.

Building stone varies in quality throughout the region and neither the predominant greywacke, nor the volcanic whinstones make good *freestone*. For this reason many towers were built of angular blocks of coursed rubble, while more easily worked sandstone was imported for doors, corners and windows, as may be seen at the towers of Aikwood (Selkirk) and Smailholm, at Neidpath Castle, in Peebles Town Wall **(Plate 14)** and the Commendator's House at Melrose Abbey. *Harling* was a common way to protect rough stonework and to emphasise the quality of freestone dressings, as may be seen at Drumlanrig's Tower. Where sandstone was plentiful in the Merse and Teviotdale, freestone ashlar could be used more extensively and left unharled, as is the case with Roxburgh Castle, parts of Cessford Castle and Littledean Tower. The quarries created in this process are no longer in operation but have made an impact on the environment through the habitats which they now provide for vegetation and animals.

Castles created a considerable demand for timber and this had a long-term effect upon the medieval woodlands. Motte and bailey castles at Hawick and elsewhere used virtually no stone and extended over a large area, as

did the pele built by King Edward I at Selkirk. Although tower houses were more economical in their use of timber because of their smaller area and use of stone vaults (normally between the first and second storeys only), upper floors and roof were generally made of wood, as were ancillary buildings. Whether or not any Borderers emulated the builders of Redesdale in Northumberland, who used oak tree trunks alone to build the walls of their "strong houses" is unclear but such houses are reported as very difficult to set alight.

Although timber stocks would be replenished in time through good woodland management, large timbers from older, taller trees would take much longer to replace. His concern for the deforestation of the lowlands induced King James I to declare stealing wood or stripping the bark from growing trees to be a crime.

Trees were cut down for other military reasons as when, in December 1317, a papal messenger found King Robert I and his men near Old Cambus (Cockburnspath) busily felling trees to construct siege engines. The sieges of Berwick, Roxburgh, Jedburgh, Wark and Norham would have impacted upon the resources of those areas to provide timber for huts, mantlets, belfreys and engines, as well as fuel for the encamped forces.

Some relatively minor repairs carried out to Newark Castle **(fig.24)** in Ettrick Forest in 1542 required the felling of enough oak trees for two joists 12m (40ft) long, as well as six sawn planks 5m (16ft) long, two timbers 4m (12ft) long and various other oak boards. Some economy is suggested by "diverr peissis of auld tymmer" and twelve "eastland" boards, presumably imported from the Baltic, hint at

Fig.24 *Newark Castle, a prominent landmark in the Yarrow Valley, was built as a stronghold of the Douglas family in the early 15th century. The tower stands inside a 16th century barmkin.*

scarcity in some types of wood. The Baltic was a particularly important source of pine for the masts and spars of ships.

Effects of war

For Borderers at the time, it was the passage of armies which made the real impact on the landscape and natural environment. Although there was little that individuals could do to protect their homes and farms against an army, they could hide themselves, their dependants and their portable goods.

A hoard of fifty-six silver coins was buried near Denholm in about 1310, which was the year when King Edward II led a force from Roxburgh into Ettrick Forest. A much larger hoard of 1,472 silver coins was concealed at Ednam in about 1321-2, when Edward was again in the Borders. On a much later

occasion, a hoard of 1,375 coins, ten of which were gold and the rest silver, was buried in a pot at Kelso. The latest of these coins was minted in the spring of 1643 and the hoard could have been buried to escape the attentions of royalist sympathisers who are known to have gathered in Kelso later that year to raise support (including money) for King Charles' cause in the Civil War.

There was an obvious impact on farmland, which may have been reduced to half its normal productivity through constant spoiling. A farm at Paxton was said in 1305 to be valueless, whereas in "time of peace" it had been worth £2-16s-8d (£2.66). However, devastation was by no means confined to farmland. In 1316 Thomas of Richmond is said to have led 10,000 men to attack a force commanded by Sir James Douglas in Jedforest and "provided them with axes to hew down the forest itself, which was one of the securest retreats of their enemies". Seventy years later John of Gaunt is reputed to have ordered the felling and burning of large areas of woodland (supposedly with 80,000 axes) in Borders and Lothian.

Nor was such devastation carried out solely at the hands of the invader. The Scots' "scorched earth" policy in 1384 was poorly received by their French allies, who on the other hand are said to have wasted timber in furnishing themselves with lodgings. In 1544 the total damage "done upon the Scots" consisted of 192 towns, towers, steads, *barmkins*, parish churches and bastell houses, 403 Scots slain, 816 prisoners, 10,386 cattle, 12,492 sheep, 1,296 horses, 200 goats and 850 bolls of corn, as well as other gear.

In the following year the Earl of Hertford reported to King Henry VIII that he had "brent (burnt), rased and cast downe" seven monasteries and friars' houses; sixteen castles, towers and peles; five market towns; 243 villages; thirteen mills and three hospitals. Hertford's raid took place in early September, so he was able to destroy or remove much of the newly-gathered harvest, which would have included seed corn for the following year.

Four years later Ralf Bulmer drew up a list of settlements along the waters of Tweed, Teviot and Ale which could be used to provide early warning and defence against a Scots attack. Of the sixty-nine settlements listed, forty had been reported destroyed by Hertford in 1545. The cost of reconstruction must have been high, especially when large timbers from mature trees were required to repair the Border abbeys. Kelso Abbey was actually abandoned

for a period during the Wars of Independence, until King David II granted the abbot permission to cut wood in Selkirk and Jedburgh Forests for rebuilding.

Clearly repairs on such a scale and with such frequency, must have had an impact on local woodland, thereby undoing any beneficial effects of forest law enforcement and good woodland management. This was also a time of increasing dependency upon livestock and much regeneration may have been suppressed by subsequent grazing.

Although much of the increase in animal (particularly sheep) husbandry was part of a wider phenomenon which had little to do with the Border wars, the situation on the border was aggravated by family feuds and reiving. Much of the work of reivers involved the rustling of cattle and sheep, which could be recovered more easily than burnt crops. Although small scale in relation to the efforts of King Edward I or the Earl of Hertford, the frequent raids from, into or within the Borders, had a cumulative effect which was quite exceptional for the time.

In the 1580s the Elliots of Liddesdale carried out more than forty raids substantially without help from other riding families and thereby rounded up more than 3,000 cattle, £1,000 worth of goods, destroyed sixty-six buildings, murdered fourteen men, and kidnapped 146 prisoners **(fig.25)**. In 1593, on the other hand the valley suffered £8,000 worth of damage, in return for £3,230 worth inflicted by Liddesdale men on the English side of the border. The unromantic reality of reiving is shown by the pettiness of the thefts. Property stolen from just one house, in 1589, included

Family Feuds

Problems posed by cross-border raiding were compounded by quarrels between families. Although feuding families often lived on different sides of the border, countrymen sometimes found themselves enemies in private wars which could last for generations.

At various points in the 16th century the Armstrongs of Liddesdale fell out with the Elliots and the Turnbulls. The Elliots, also of Liddesdale, were enemies of the Pringles of the Galashiels area and the Scotts of Teviotdale. The Turnbulls of Minto were at feud with the Kerrs, who in turn were at odds with the Scotts, the Rutherfords, the town of Jedburgh, and even other branches of the Kerr family.

Feuds grew out of the desire for revenge, and a single incident could spark off a vendetta which would endure for years, in much the same way as the Montagues and Capulets of "Romeo and Juliet". The Scott-Kerr feud began with a skirmish on the banks of the Tweed at Melrose in 1526, when Kerr of Cessford was killed. Ill feeling festered, however, and a generation later revenge was exacted when Scott of Buccleuch was murdered in Edinburgh High Street by a gang of Kerrs in 1552. After this the two families were reconciled by marriage alliances and private treaties.

Fig.25 Family feuds

a woman's dress, handkerchiefs, underclothes, sheets, shirts and four children's coats.

The Border wars coincided with a marked decline in the extent of woodland cover, particularly in the valleys of Yarrow, Ettrick and Jed. However, if deliberate deforestation took place on the scale which medieval writers suggest (and this is difficult to believe) trees would still have regenerated though natural processes. That this did not happen was probably due to the economic basis of the wars, which placed great emphasis on the taxes levied on wool, export of which also paid for foreign munitions. Melrose Abbey alone owned some 22,000 acres of land, much of which was given over to large flocks of sheep, and in 1328 wool exported through Berwick accounted for about one third of Scotland's total. Although sheep did not cut down trees

they, more than any other agency, have suppressed regeneration and in this way maintain the Border hills as open moorland.

Two other animals added to the problem. Rabbits had been introduced as a food source by the Normans, who farmed them in specially constructed warrens. Escaped rabbits not only affected growing crops, but also caused severe soil erosion. The influence of the black rat was rather different, for, in 1349, it introduced the Black Death into Scotland. Believing that Scotland had been spared the fate which had already befallen England (where a third of the population may have died) a Scottish army assembled in Ettrick Forest to take advantage of the situation. The plague made its first appearance north of the Border among the ranks of the soldiery and it spread through the land, although its impact was probably reduced among Scotland's more dispersed population.

The very people who knew how to manage woods included those Ettrick foresters who no doubt provided many of the archers for Scotland's medieval armies. The death of such people, either as casualties in war or as victims of the Black Death and other plagues, would have had consequences for the future of Borders' forests.

War, plague and farming conspired against the remaining woodlands of the Borders, to provide a legacy of open moorland where trees formerly grew. Not only did they cause the disappearance of those woods but they suppressed any attempts by trees to re-establish themselves.

As well as the contribution to the wider landscape, warfare or disorder have left behind an abundance of ruins and many of these now provide habitats for plants and animals. Tiny droppings on floors can betray colonies of Daubenton's or Pipestrelle bats in the ceilings above, while house martins and swallows – the "temple-haunting martlets" of Macbeth - arrive each summer to build their nests in arches and overhangs. Walls attract a variety of plants, not least ivy, and the whole appearance of some buildings can be altered by the growth of lichens, particularly the orange coloured *Xanthoria parietina* which favours a number of Borders towers.

In the 20th century two World Wars made inroads on Borders woodlands, just as they did in the rest of Britain. One result was the foundation of the Forestry Commission and the growth of public forests to recoup the losses. Although the vast majority are non-native species such as Sitka Spruce, the Borders now contains far more trees than at any time since the Middle Ages.

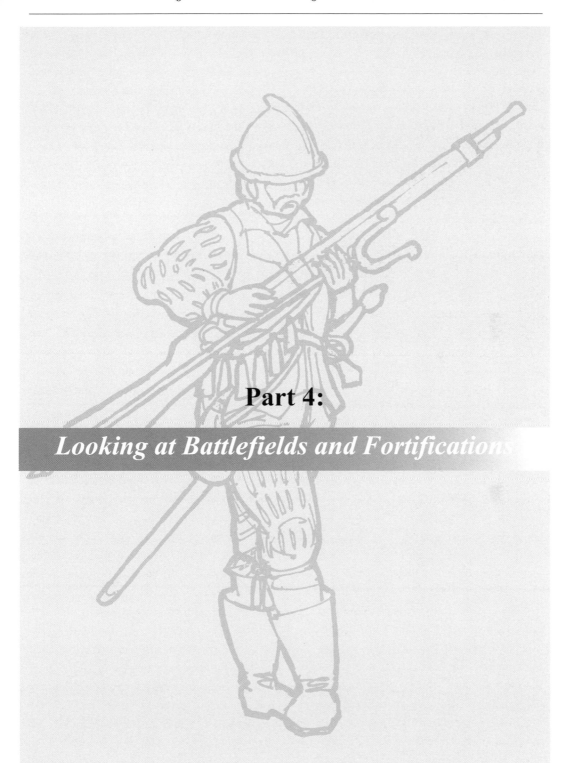

Part 4:

Looking at Battlefields and Fortifications

Part 4: Looking at Battlefields and Fortifications

Visitors to the Borders have a real opportunity to explore places where history was made. The great battles of Bannockburn and Flodden may have taken place outside the region but the armies which fought in them first passed through the Borders. No comparable area in Scotland can claim a richer heritage of towers and castles.

Battlefields

Although the Borders have seen the passage of many armies, most of the places where they fought offer little for today's visitor. Places such as Skirmish Field (Melrose), Englishman's Syke (Galashiels), Hornshole (Hawick) and Barefoots (Eyemouth) are traditionally identified with fighting but contemporary chronicles give little or no information concerning the events which happened there. Even where the course of the battle can be related to a specific place, as at Ancrum Moor or Philiphaugh, access to the battlefield may be restricted, since most sites are in private ownership.

The battle of **Degsastan (AD603)** would scarcely have compared with a skirmish a thousand years later. However, to Áedán mac Gabhráin, king of Dalriada and Aethelfrith, king of Bernicia, the fight was a decisive moment in their struggle for power in the Southern Uplands. Not much is known of the battle, but their war bands are believed to have met in the wild valley of the Dawston Burn at the head of Liddesdale, close to the point where the road from Kielder Water and North Tynedale enters Scotland.

The Anglian force was led by Hering, son of Hussa the previous king and included Aethelfrith's brother Theobald. He was a subordinate commander who perished with his followers. The Scotti fared worse, as almost the whole force was wiped out, and Áedán's son Domingart was probably among those killed. The medieval Anglo-Saxon Chronicle records that "never since has any Scottish king dared to lead an army into this nation".

The battle of **Ancrum Moor (1545)** arose from an expedition led by the Warden of the English Middle March, Sir Ralph Eure, who had ravaged Jedburgh and Kelso with the help of some families of Border Scots in the previous year. His opponent was the Earl of Angus, who had fought with the English at Hadden Rigg in 1542, but had been on the Scottish side in an attack on Coldingham Priory in 1544.

Angus now sought to punish those Borderers who were fighting with Eure, who in turn tried a pre-emptive night strike on Angus at Melrose to protect them. Outnumbered, Angus avoided battle, but shadowed Eure's force as it harried the district and made its way back towards Jedburgh along the Roman road, Dere Street. Pausing to burn a tower (reputedly with an old lady and her family still inside), the English force of 3,000 men retired towards the ridge known as Lilliardsedge. By this time Angus had been reinforced, and had set an ambush for the English on the blind side of the ridge. Caught unawares, Eure's chances of victory vanished as his reiver allies changed sides. He and hundreds of his men were killed and more than a thousand were taken prisoner.

Today the site can best be seen from the Dere Street footpath (part of St. Cuthbert's Way: **fig.16**). Beside the path there is an inscription dedicated to the maid Lillyard, a mythical combatant:

Fair Maiden Lillyard lies under this stane;
Little was her stature, but great was
her fame;
Upon the English louns she laid
many thumps,
and when her legs were smitten off,
she fought upon her stumps.

The ridge was known as Lilliardsedge long before the battle, and Lyliot's Cross, where the Scottish and English peace commissioners met in 1379 and 1383, may have occupied the site before the present stone.

A meeting of the March Wardens on the border at Carter Bar was the occasion for the **Redeswire Fray (1575)**. The English Warden, Sir John Forster, met with the Keeper of Liddesdale, Sir John Carmichael to hear and judge accusations brought forward on both sides. A disagreement between these two escalated into an armed brawl between their supporters. The Northumberland men started to use their bows, but the arrival of Jedburgh men was decisive. The fray ended with the deputy English Warden being killed, Forster and others being taken prisoner, and the Scots in possession of the field.

This was not only a battle, but also an international incident which was resolved by higher authority on both sides before it could lead to renewed war. Carter Bar provides a spectacular first view of Scotland for visitors crossing the border, and the open ground to

the east of the road is where the events took place.

The Borders saw little action in the Civil War, where there was hardly any popular support for the king's cause beyond that provided by some landowners, notably the lairds of Traquair, Roxburghe and Hume. After a series of dazzling successes in the north, the Marquis of Montrose brought a depleted force south in an attempt to swell its numbers, but suffered his first defeat at **Philiphaugh (1645)**. Unaware that a force commanded by Sir David Leslie was on his trail, Montrose and his cavalry were quartered in Selkirk, but his cannon and infantry were across the valley near Philiphaugh House. Leslie's force reached the scene in September mist and took the royalists by surprise with attacks to their flank and front. By the time Montrose arrived the battle was lost so he made his escape and sought refuge at Traquair House.

Leslie's victory was concluded when Montrose's Irish infantry surrendered with their wives and children. Such was the hatred between the opposing sides that, although their safety had been assured, the captives were all killed, reputedly in the courtyard of Newark Castle and on a nearby piece of ground which is still known as Slain Men's Lea (Selkirk).

The Border abbeys all suffered in the wars, and the destruction is sometimes visible in their fabric or in the rebuilding which took place afterwards. **Coldingham Priory** may have been rebuilt after an attack by King John of England and was certainly considered for fortification - and defended - during the Rough Wooing. It survived these conflicts only to be blown up by Oliver Cromwell during the Civil

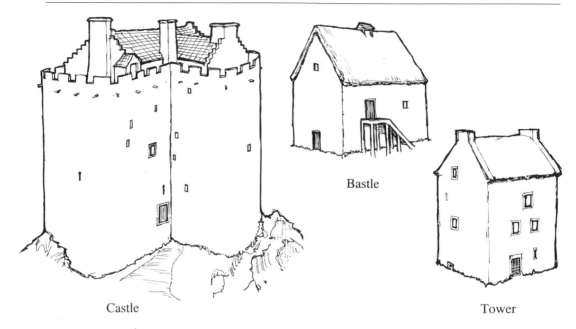

Castle   Bastle   Tower

Fig.26 By the 16th century fortified homes varied greatly in scale and quality, and the distinction between castles and other towers is far from clear. A wall walk at roof level was a basic requirement of a castle, but some particularly grand towers lacked one. The bastle or "pele house" was a fortified farmhouse and can be distinguished from a tower in its longer, lower profile. Even so, any ruined fortified house may have the name "tower" or "castle".

War. **Melrose Abbey** church was rebuilt after its devastation by King Richard II in 1385. **Jedburgh Abbey** was actually fortified by the French and held against the English in 1548. **Jedburgh Greyfriars** (now visible only as foundations in a public garden) was destroyed in 1545 by English gunners, whose stone cannon balls were found during its excavation. The sack of **Kelso Abbey** by Spanish troops in 1545 provides a particularly vivid image, recorded in the Earl of Hertford's correspondence, of the nature of Border warfare.

Fortifications

Although soldiers made use of ground and non-military buildings when fighting, they occupied and defended buildings designed for the purpose whenever possible and the Borders has a rich heritage of fortifications.

The first castles were built in the 12th century as fortified homes for the king and for the barons and knights who made up his feudal tenants. Royal castles were home to *constables*, who administered the royal estates on behalf of the king in his absence. The social role of the king and his aristocratic tenants meant that the castle was also an administrative workplace. Peebles, Selkirk, Roxburgh and Berwick were all royal castles and the constables appointed to them were also sheriffs with responsibility for the administration of the dependent counties. Castles were also a status symbol and it was not until the 15th and 16th centuries that a rising middle class began to fortify their homes **(fig.26)**.

Earthwork castles

Although important as status symbols, fortifications were not just for show but intended to provide real security. Many of these early castles were earth and timber and consisted of two parts: a motte, or mound supporting a timber tower for the owner and his family, and a bailey, or courtyard to accommodate his household.

The royal motte and bailey castle at Selkirk is not accessible to the public, nor are the baronial strongholds of Walter de Riddale at Lilliesleaf, Ranulph de Soules at Liddel Castle (Castleton), nor Fast Castle on the Balliol estate of Cavers. At Hawick, however, the castle of the Lovel family is represented by Hawick Mote, a motte almost 8m (25ft) high in Moat Park, where the earthworks of the bailey have long since been levelled (**fig.3**). The castle of the de Morville family probably stood at Lauder but its earthworks would long since have been obscured, firstly by the construction of an artillery fort in the 16th century and subsequently by Thirlestane Castle and its gardens. At Hermitage the 13th century castle of the de Soules family may be represented by earthworks which surround the later stone tower.

Early stone castles

Sometime around 1128 the royal castle of Roxburgh consisted of an enclosure containing the Church of St. John and a tower or donjon. In the 12th century novel, 'Roman de Fergus', the hero's lover is besieged in Roxburgh Castle, which we are told, possessed a square *keep*, a church and a *postern*. Although the castle underwent many subsequent changes

and has now virtually disappeared, it is clear that here King David I had a stone castle with a keep and *curtain wall* instead of an earthwork motte and palisade. This happened throughout the lands settled by the Normans and keep and bailey castles can still be seen at Carlisle and Norham on the English side of the Border.

A later account of the condition of the castle makes it plain that by the early 15th century a number of towers, at least one of which was round, had been added to the curtain wall. This reflects a more aggressive approach to castle design than that which had been developed in the Crusades.

Men attacking early castles were vulnerable to arrows and other missiles as they approached the walls, although they reduced the chance of being hit by spreading out. Once at the foot of the wall they were relatively safe from the defenders, who had to lean out over the *parapet* to fire at or drop things on them. In doing so the defenders became targets for the attackers' archers. By adding towers to the wall, archers not only remained under cover themselves but were able to enfilade, or fire along a grouped target of men gathered at the base of the wall (**fig.27**). Another solution to this problem was the construction of a projecting gallery or *bretasche* along the wall-head directly over the foot of the curtain. The *corbels* and sockets for supporting such a timber gallery can be seen in the late 14th century walls of Hermitage Castle.

The records of towers at Roxburgh show that the early castle was strengthened at different times and mention of a round tower (implying that others, like the keep, were square), reflects another military innovation. Square towers

Building for Active Defence

Medieval Castle Walls

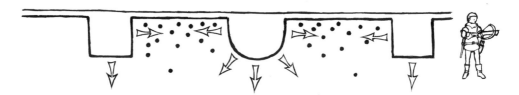

Renaissance Artillery Fortifications

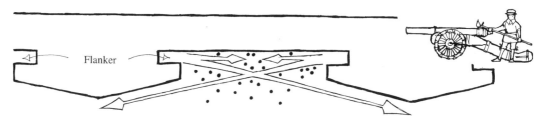

Flanker

Fig.27 Military engineers created opportunities to catch attackers in cross fire where they provided a concentrated target. Castle builders of the 13th century did this by adding flanking towers to the walls, but during the 16th century Renaissance engineers designed pointed bastions with concealed guns in flankers and these were even more effective.

were added to curtain walls in the 12th century but proved to be vulnerable to undermining. In the 13th century stronger round towers were preferred as there were fewer "blind spots" for archers firing from them and they were more resistant to undermining. Walls with round towers were still being built in the 15th and 16th centuries at Tinnis Castle (Drumelzier) and around the burgh of Peebles, where one still survives.

A strong gatehouse and high walls flanked by towers were designed to keep out attackers so effectively that a donjon, or final refuge was unnecessary. Castles of this kind reached their ultimate form in the series of great fortresses which King Edward I of England built in north Wales between 1277 and 1298. Following the death of King Alexander III, Edward turned his attention to Scotland and brought with him

his military engineer, Master James of St. George. By this time, however, he no longer had the money for building on the Welsh scale and built no large castles, although he did introduce another form of defence.

In Wales Edward protected his building projects by means of a palisaded enclosure, which he now introduced into Scotland at Selkirk, Lochmaben and Linlithgow as strongholds for garrisons. This form of defence was called a pele (derived from French word for stake: *pel*) and at Selkirk it included a tower with a postern faced with stone, a stone gatehouse with drawbridge and 285 metres of timber palisade (enough for an enclosure 70m square, or about one acre). The pele probably occupied the site of the earlier royal motte and bailey castle, which stands on private ground just outside the town centre.

Hume Castle belongs to a class of simple, broadly rectangular, walled enclosures which were built from the 12th century onwards by landowners with more modest resources than the king or his chief nobles. Today the castle is an imaginative reconstruction built in 1794 on the original curtain wall to provide a landmark for miles around **(Plate 11)**. The walls certainly provide stunning views across the Merse and it is easy to see why the castle was deemed to be of great value by Scottish and English alike.

The main interest in the castle consists of the rather stark form, without towers and almost without windows, of the curtain wall on its rocky volcanic crag. Beside the restored entrance doorway this curtain is pierced by a dumbbell-shaped gun-loop, which may date from the later 14th or early 15th century. It is recorded that steps were again taken to fortify Hume with artillery in 1481. The high ground level inside the castle has built up over and around the remains of internal structures, which include a well and one wall of a central tower or keep.

Hume played a central role in 16th century campaigns through its strategic command of the Merse. Although it was an objective of Hertford's raid of 1545, he did not capture it until after the Battle of Pinkie two years later. It was recovered by Alexander Home in 1549 but twenty years later was battered into surrender by the guns of the Earl of Sussex. In 1650 Colonels Fenwick and Syler of Cromwell's army once more bombarded the castle and its seventy-five-strong garrison into submission, using mortars and a *culverin*. Although, in keeping with Cromwellian policy, the castle is said to have been

demolished after this, a barracks may have existed there in 1745, when the people of Kelso asked for the use of its cannon. The restored walls were once again used for defence in the Napoleonic Wars, when they supported a warning beacon. It was from Hume that a false alarm was sent out in 1804 after a bonfire in the Cheviot hills was mistaken for the invasion signal.

Development of the tower

Although the term pele had a specific meaning in the early 14th century, it came in time to be applied not only to a defended enclosure but more particularly to the tower which stood within it. The tower house was popular in Scotland, northern England and Ireland from the 14th to the 17th century. In the Borders, tower building reached its peak in the 16th century and in 1535 King James V decreed that each man with a hundred pounds worth of land was to build a barmkin for safety of humans and stock. Many of the ruined towers of the Borders countryside were built after this decree. During this period, the history of castles and castle building followed rather different courses in England and Scotland.

Invasions of the northern counties of England by Scottish armies in the 14th century stemmed the general tendency of English castle builders to pay increasing attention to comfort at the expense of strength. Here powerful nobles such as the Nevilles of Raby and the Scropes of Bolton arranged their living accommodation in corner towers and high connecting ranges around a central courtyard. Their followers could not afford to build on this scale and so the courtyard was moved outside, along with some of the service buildings and the accommodation was reduced in size to fit a single tower. This arrangement is well represented at Etal Castle (Northumberland) near Coldstream.

The nobility of Scotland continued to build castles but in the Borders few survive from the 14th and 15th centuries. During the English wars of the mid-14th century **Hermitage Castle (front cover)** changed hands several times and was twice in the possession of the Neville family. The present stone castle originated at this time as a manor house in the English style with a central courtyard. It was acquired and enlarged by the powerful Douglas family, who closed in and converted it into a large rectangular tower entered at first floor level through a small rectangular gate turret. By the 15th century four rectangular corner towers had been added (perhaps inspired by the castles of Haughton, Tarset and Dally across the border in North Tynedale), with a continuous timber gallery built out from the wall-head on stone corbels. Today the building is entered from a later door at ground level and 16th century gun-loops have been inserted in the walls.

The unusually large amount of accommodation in the tower at Hermitage, while no doubt being a reflection of the owner's wealth, may have been necessary to make up for the lack of an external courtyard. The broadly contemporary but smaller towers of Newark, Neidpath and Cessford possessed space in the courtyard for additional domestic accommodation.

Newark Castle (fig.24: not open to the public) was built early in the 15th century and provided the Earls of Douglas with a base from which to operate in Tweeddale and Teviotdale. It dominates the eastern end of the Yarrow Valley and consists of a plain rectangular tower which has been stripped of most of its freestone dressings. Here only the basement was vaulted but high enough to accommodate an additional *entresol* floor within the vault. As at Hermitage, access was originally at first floor level, which was linked by spiral stairs to the basement and upper storeys.

Ancillary buildings would have existed around the tower, as excavations have revealed at another Douglas castle at Threave (Dumfries and Galloway), but any early enclosure was replaced in the 16th century by a stone walled barmkin pierced by oval loops for hand guns. In the 17th century, when security was less important, an entry to the tower was made at ground level.

Neidpath Castle (Plate 4) is a magnificent stronghold of the Hay family. Its site was carefully chosen to take advantage of a rocky perch above the River Tweed, where a narrow gorge allowed it to dominate the main route west from Peebles. The design was adapted to the site, with rounded external corners and no wall angle is square. The massively thick walls enclosed five chambers in the main part of the castle, six smaller ones in the wing and contained several more within their thickness.

Access was via a door at ground level, with a secondary postern door reached by wooden steps; both had adjoining guard chambers. A prison occupied the lowest level of the wing, stores were kept in the main chamber, and on a wooden floor within the stone vault. The hall and kitchen were on the first floor and reached by a spiral staircase. Above this level were bedchambers and the battlements. Stables and other supporting buildings have long gone, but their place is occupied by a series of later buildings, the earliest of which is 16th or 17th century.

In 1645 the castle was held for Parliament against Montrose's forces, before their defeat at Philiphaugh. The ruinous wing is said to date from the time of Cromwell's campaign of 1650, but contemporary accounts suggest that the garrison surrendered without the need for a bombardment.

The rounded corners on Neidpath Castle may be designed for strength but by avoiding square corners, the builders reduced the amount of expensive freestone which was needed for *quoins*. This type of construction was also used in the three Berwickshire towers of Cranshaws (Longformacus), Corsbie (Legerwood) and Evelaw (Westruther).

Although the ruins of **Cessford Castle (Plate 5)** are not open to the public, they are readily visible from St. Cuthbert's Way. They consist of a strong L-shaped tower which stands within the remains of a walled courtyard. The stonework suggests that the tower had an interrupted building history, which is not surprising in view of the events which took place there. Its involvement in the Border wars led to various structural alterations to its massive 4m (13ft) thick walls and in its present state it consists of a main block with a wing to the east. Doors were provided at ground floor and first floor level in the angle of the L. In addition to vaults at two levels, the main block also housed wooden entresol floors and three *mural chambers*. The wing stood five or six storeys high with a pit prison at the bottom

and kitchen and other chambers above.

The castle was probably built between 1446 and 1467 by Andrew Ker of Altonburn (Morebattle) and became the family seat of the house of Ker of Cessford, from which a number of Wardens of the Middle March were drawn. In 1482 it is reported to have had a garrison of sixty men and subsequently saw considerable involvement in Border affairs.

It was "cast down" by the English in 1519 and the subject of a remarkable siege in 1523, when an English force under the Earl of Surrey brought a battery of eleven cannon to bear on its walls. Under cover of archers and cannon, Surrey's men scaled the walls of the "barbican" but were unable to gain entry to the great tower. They brought two culverins to bear against a blocked up window and when the gunners had made an entry into the chamber behind, they intended to blow up the tower with four barrels of gunpowder. The defenders set fire to the powder before the mine was ready and three of the gunners were badly burned. The siege ended when the owner, Sir Andrew Ker arrived and agreed to hand over the castle on condition that he was allowed to remove his possessions. He regained his castle when the English force withdrew from Teviotdale later that year. Cessford again suffered from English invasions in 1543, 1544 and 1545 but it continued to be the family seat until Sir Robert Ker, who later became Earl of Roxburghe, acquired the former lands of Kelso Abbey in 1607 and moved to the house of Fleurs (later Floors Castle).

The Pringle stronghold of **Smailholm Tower (Plate 6)** is a smaller building than the castles just described but occupies an exceptionally

Medieval Smailholm

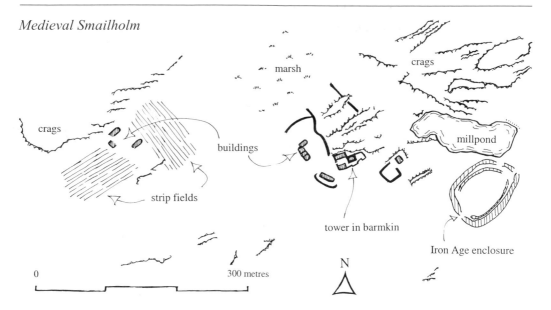

Fig.28 *Stone towers seldom stood on their own, and at Smailholm Crags the tower can be seen in relation to its landscape. Smailholm Tower stands within a walled barmkin with the remains of a hall and kitchen block, while around are the sites of other dwellings, enclosures, strip fields and a millpond.*

prominent location in the Borders landscape, as it sits high on a rock outcrop with extensive views in all directions. George Pringle was master ranger in Ettrick Forest in the middle years of the 15th century and may have modelled the tower on Newark Castle, which was the home of his feudal superiors, the Douglases.

The settlement of Smailholm suffered during the Rough Wooing and traces of rectangular buildings and walled enclosures can be made out in the surrounding turf. These are the last remains of the hamlet which clustered around the tower **(fig.28)**. Such settlements would have accompanied most rural towers. Andrew Pringle transferred his principal home to Galashiels in 1574 and his descendent sold the Smailholm estate to the Scotts of Harden in 1645. Today the tower contains a series of miniature tableaux which celebrate the literary works of Sir Walter Scott.

The tower stands within a walled barmkin and is built of basalt with sandstone dressings. It is a plain rectangular building of five floors linked by a spiral stair and entered at ground level. There are battlements on two sides between *crowstepped* gables. The entrance to the barmkin leads to the west courtyard, where excavations have revealed the remains of domestic buildings of the kind which were normal elements of a tower complex but have usually disappeared without trace. On the north side was a hall block which might suggest that, like some medieval castles, the owner preferred to live outside the tower. On the south side were two rooms with fireplaces which were likely to have been where cooking, brewing and other such activities were carried out. The remaining space enclosed by the 1m (3ft) thick barmkin wall consists of an eastern courtyard, which may have been used as a garden.

Border Towers in the 16th century

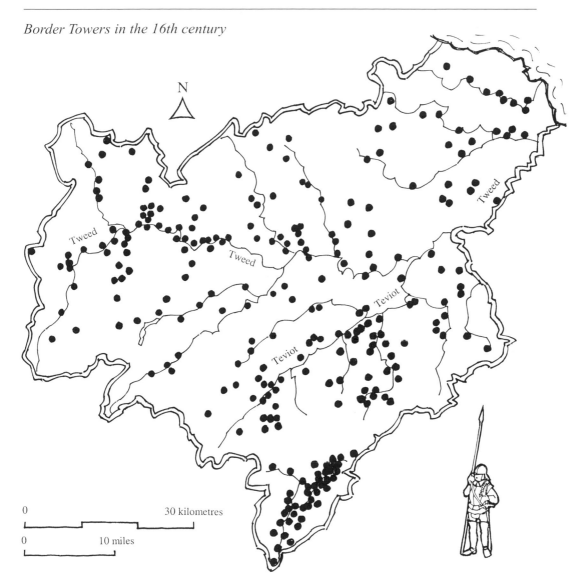

Fig.29 *Lawlessness and constant raiding, rather than invading armies, led to the construction of towers and bastles throughout the region in the 16th century. Liddesdale "riding" families were such active reivers that their valley was heavily fortified against reprisals.*

Later towers

The towers already described were built in the days when bowmen still dominated the battlefield. In the 16th century increasing use of firearms coincided with the ability of more families to build towers, with the result that gun-loops became common features of Borders defensive architecture. At the same time, the kinds of towers which had developed in the 14th and 15th centuries still provided the basic pattern for the homes of prospering families **(fig.29)**.

Defences of Greenknowe Tower

Fig.30 *The designer of Greenknowe Tower provided almost all-round protection against attack through liberal provision of shot holes and gun loops with overlapping fields of fire.*

As towers increased significantly in numbers, it became possible to send warning from one to another in time of danger. In Tweeddale, for example, there were some sixteen smaller towers between the castles of Neidpath and Elibank (Caddonfoot), a distance of 23km (14 miles). In Liddesdale, however, which was notorious for the reivers who lived in the valley, there were more than twice as many towers for the same distance – a reflection of their position right on the frontier with England. These have almost all now disappeared, and surviving clusters of towers at Colmslie (three) and Darnick (two), both in Melrose parish, are not a true reflection of where defences were originally distributed.

In its developed 16th century form **Drumlanrig's Tower (Plate 16)** was an L-plan building, with a vaulted basement and a wall walk at roof level. The ground floor door had been in the *re-entrant angle* and was

covered by a gun-loop for a hand gun and another loop covered the Slitrig Water side of the building. The tower was one of at least three in Hawick and was extended to build the town house of the Duchess of Buccleuch in the late 17th century. Although later alterations have obscured or removed many original features, the tower now houses a visitor centre which gives a vivid picture of reiving in 16th century Teviotdale.

The tower belonged to the Douglases of Drumlanrig in Dumfriesshire, but by 1570, when an English force raided the district, it had been forcibly taken over by Scott of Buccleuch. The raiders were frustrated by the townspeople who pulled the thatch off their roofs and burned it in the street, so that the thick smoke prevented the English from entering the town. At Douglas' request the tower, and all the goods brought to it for safety, were spared "for honour's sake".

Fig.31 Aikwood Tower, built in the late 16th or early 17th century, is a substantial tower with cap houses but no battlement walk. Seen here before restoration.

The Buccleuchs continued to use the tower as their base (for raiding England among other things), and in 1596 the rescue of Kinmont Willie Armstrong (a prisoner in Carlisle Castle) may have been planned there. Even after the Border wars had ended, the tower saw further action when it was seized during an armed rising of several hundred Covenanters in 1679.

The finest Borders example of the developed L-plan is **Greenknowe Tower (Plate 7)**, which was built in 1581 for James Seton of Touch and Jane Edmonstone his wife, who are commemorated by a date stone and coats of arms over the door. The entrance, protected by an iron *yett*, is again at ground level and placed in the re-entrant angle, where it could be covered from the adjoining vaulted cellar.

One gun-loop close to the ground in the wing is positioned to rake the ground in front, although a paved area indicates that there was an external building in this direction. There are four main floors, the first of which is reached by a main stair in the wing, while a smaller turret stair occupies the re-entrant angle from first floor level. Architectural details include *string courses*, corbelled turrets (with shot holes to cover the wall foot on each side: **fig.30**), crowstepped gables and fireplaces. The use of straining arches to spread the weight of masonry above fireplace, door and window lintels is well exhibited here.

Recently restored, **Aikwood (fig.31)** is a good example of a plain, rectangular plan tower which enabled a branch of the Scott family to dominate access along the lower Ettrick valley. The name of the tower recalls that oak trees were more plentiful in the past than today. The door has its original knocker or "risp" and leads to a vaulted basement with a spiral stair which gives access to the hall above and three upper floors. Although there are *cap houses* at two corners, there is no wall walk. Shot holes for pistols include at least one which was for show only.

Today the tower is adjoined by the James Hogg Centre which celebrates the literary works of the "Ettrick Shepherd". The tower features in Border tradition as the home of Michael Scott the Wizard and also of Will Scott, the husband of Muckle Mou'd Meg Murray of Elibank.

As they acquired the means to do so, some landed families chose to make their homes larger and more comfortable. The result was country houses which paid much less attention to the prospect of a siege, and more to greater convenience, although they still often carry the name "tower". Such was the case with **Traquair House**, home of the Stewarts of Traquair, and reputedly the oldest continuously inhabited house in Scotland. The 16th century mansion encloses a 15th century tower, which is hidden from view by the harled exterior. Internally the three storey tower still retains a stair in the thickness of the wall and secret quarters for the Roman Catholic priest who served the family through periods of persecution. Traquair is a treasure, as it has been altered little since the 17th century, when the Stewarts played a leading role in politics and the Earl of Traquair was King Charles I's Lord Treasurer in Scotland. More than any other building in the area it creates the atmosphere of a large house as Borderers of the reiving period would have known it.

Thirlestane Castle was built to a most unusual design at the end of the 16th century and occupies the site of the abandoned English artillery fort of Lauder. Like Traquair House and the unfinished Drochil Castle, long suites of rooms are arranged on several levels to provide a much greater standard of comfort than more traditional tower houses. As built, Thirlestane was long and narrow with round towers at each corner, turrets along the narrow sides and a wall walk which gave the structure a martial appearance. The building was later modified and the interior is notable for its 17th century plaster ceilings which emphasise the owner's concern for comfort. The castle was host to Bonnie Prince Charlie after the Battle of Prestonpans in 1745.

Andrew Pringle and his wife Mariota Borthwick also opted for comfort when they built **Old Gala House** in or about 1583 to replace an earlier tower house. They replaced the earlier tower with a simple building of two storeys and an attic which subsequently became the east wing of a larger house built in about 1611. The 17th century house contains a fine painted ceiling which bears the initials of Hugh Scott and Jean Pringle his wife, together with the date 1635. Further extended in the 18th and 19th centuries, the house formed the home of the Scotts of Gala and is now a museum.

Bastles

The move towards comfort can also be seen in **Mary, Queen of Scots House** at Jedburgh **(Plate 12)**, which seems to have begun life as a *bastle* house. In its original form it consisted of a vaulted basement with a hall above and an attic storey. The upper storeys were reached by an external wooden stair but this was replaced in the 17th century when an eastern range was added with a spiral stair in its lowest storey and a smaller stair turret above (much in the manner of Greenknowe Tower).

Mary leased a house from Lady Ferniehirst for forty pounds in 1566 and visited her lover Bothwell at Hermitage while she was in residence. Although tradition says that this was the building now known as Mary, Queen of Scots House, there were at least six towers in Jedburgh in the 16th century, and the coat of arms over the doorway suggests that this tower belonged to the Wigmer family. Even so, the stairs all turn to the left, which is a characteristic of buildings owned by the Kerr family. The Kerrs were famously left-handed and this design meant that they could use their swords if called upon to defend the stairs. The house is now a museum and among the

Communal Defence on the Border

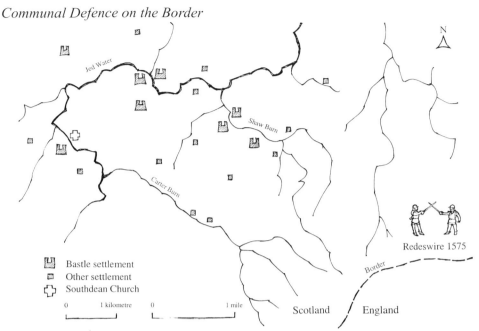

Fig.32 *By the 16th century border warfare and raiding had become a way of life in the upper Jed Water valley, where the Otterburn campaign had been planned in Southdean Church in 1388. Fortified farmhouses (bastles) delayed or discouraged reiving bands and allowed time for neighbours to organise resistance. Settlements on the English side of the border mirror this pattern and emphasise that no side enjoyed a monopoly on reiving. The Redeswire Fray broke out at a meeting to address grievances from both sides of the border.*

artefacts on view is a dagger from the battlefield of Carberry Hill (Midlothian) and a 16th century French cannon from Ferniehirst Castle.

The bastle **(fig.26)** is a characteristic frontier building type of which very few examples still survive on the Scottish side of the Border. Based upon the medieval hall house, the bastle was longer than it was tall and consisted of three storeys. An unlit basement, sometimes vaulted but generally not, was entered at ground level and although it was used for storage it was also capable of sheltering people and animals in times of need. The hall or living room above was entered by a separate door and reached by an external wooden stair which could be removed as necessary. Windows at

this level were few and very small. There may have been access to the basement by a trapdoor, or occasionally an internal stair. The attic level could be little more than a roofed in space but may have provided sleeping accommodation. The walls were immensely thick and the doorways were more like passages in their own right.

Although such buildings have been recognised well into the Southern Uplands, in the Borders the surviving examples are in Teviotdale or in the valleys of its tributaries. Marked on maps as "pele houses", they closely resemble Northumberland bastles, from which they may well be copied. **Kilnsike Tower** (Southdean: **Plate 13)** is such a building and is readily visible from the public road, although it is not

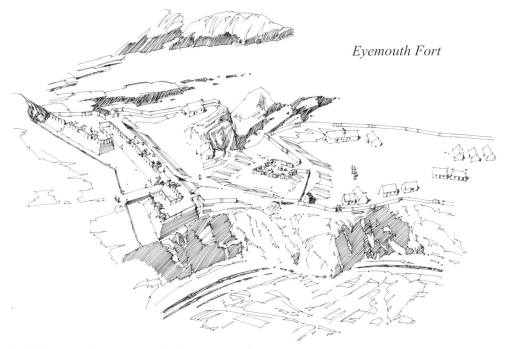

Fig.33 Eyemouth Fort as it might have appeared under French occupation in 1558. The engineer who designed the fort incorporated the earthworks of the earlier English fort as a second line of gun emplacements. Drawing by Dave Pollock.

open to the public. These buildings were fortified farms and a series of them can be traced, either as sites or as standing remains, along the course of the upper Jed Water **(fig.32)**. Here the Olivers and other families once perched on the very edge of the kingdom and exchanged reiving bouts with their English neighbours of Redesdale to the south. Although these houses lacked battlements, they were close enough together to attract the attention of neighbours when a raid was under way.

Artillery fortifications

Although castle building in England ceased during the 15th century, the impact of artillery on traditional fortifications led to a long period of adjustment, when castles such as Carlisle, Wark, Norham and Berwick were modified to take the new weapons. This work was carried out by the Crown, or by powerful landowners acting in the national interest, for use in time of war. The most successful responses to cannon were undoubtedly the specially built forts which were designed from the start to resist artillery with artillery. On the English side of the border, the outstanding example of this and still exceptional in England as a whole, is the walls of Berwick **(fig.20 & Plate 10)**. These include not only the bastioned *trace* designed by Sir Richard Lee in 1557 but the earlier Lord's Mount gun tower which was built in response to the invasion scare of 1539, when the whole of King Henry VIII's kingdom was threatened with attack by the forces of France and Spain.

On the Scottish side of the border **Eyemouth Fort (fig.33 & Plate 9)** provides not only the best example of such fortifications in the Borders but also one of the earliest surviving examples in Britain of the Italian school of fortress design. The remains of two forts, built in 1547 and 1557, can be seen. They occupy a rocky promontory with a rampart across its neck.

The first fort was designed by Sir Richard Lee and his work can still be followed on the ground. This consisted of a "W" plan ditch in front of a central pointed bastion between two lengths of rampart. The ramparts were angled forward and provided with gun emplacements to cover the faces of the bastion, while two guns in each flank of the bastion covered the fronts of the ramparts. A contemporary plan shows a series of internal buildings which housed the garrison and state papers provide details of the armament and garrison. The disadvantage of Lee's chosen design was that the guns placed in the rampart to cover the bastion were themselves exposed to an attacker's cannon, and by enclosing only a part of the headland Lee left room for attackers to set up guns on a small promontory outside the walls.

During the construction of the second fort, the French engineer, possibly Jean Roytell, enclosed the whole headland with a single straight curtain with bastions or half-bastions at each end and a ditch in front. There may have been a *glacis*, or raised slope, in front of the defences designed to reduce the target which they presented to enemy gunfire. The strength of the French design was that guns positioned in the flanks of the bastions could catch any attackers in a cross-fire as they crossed the ditch and prepared to scale the rampart, while the guns themselves were recessed and not exposed to the attackers' cannon fire **(fig.27)**. At the same time, guns on the rampart, or on Lee's earlier bastion (now refurbished as a *cavalier*) could direct a sweeping fire over the glacis.

The records suggest that the French supplied the fort with more guns and men than had been available to Lee. This was probably because the French occupied a post which was nearer to the enemy than any of their other strongholds, whereas Lee's fort, although in hostile territory, was one of the nearest to friendly territory.

The forts built at Eyemouth were relatively cheap because they involved very little masonry and consisted mainly of earthworks. As little more than picks, shovels and a labour force were needed to construct effective protection against cannon fire, smaller field works began to make their appearance on the battlefield.

Although its construction and landscaping have removed any traces, **Paxton House** stands on the site of a fortified *bridgehead*. This was constructed in 1639 for King Charles I's army, which occupied a large entrenched camp on the English bank of the Tweed. In this campaign Charles' forces were opposed by an army which encamped on Duns Law.

The Scots force was commanded by Alexander Leslie, who was a veteran of the Thirty Years War then being waged on the continent. He had been a Field Marshal in the Swedish army, had successfully defended Stralsund in 1628 and had fought at the battle of Lützen in 1632.

His base at Duns is still marked by the Covenanters' Stone (a rough boulder on the hill top where the standard is said to have been raised) and the **Covenanters' Redoubt**. This latter occupies an area of the summit some 60m square and is enclosed by a low, narrow earthwork with small bastions at each corner **(Plate 15)**. Although nothing like the scale of the earthworks at Eyemouth, this was essentially a temporary field work which would have been augmented by a wooden *breastwork*, or perhaps earth-filled *gabions* and would have provided a rallying point for troops in battle. Each front would have been covered by cross fire from the small corner bastions. Small circular banked enclosures close to the edge of the flat summit could have been additional gun emplacements with a better command of the hill slopes.

John Aston was part of an embassy from King Charles to Leslie and has left an account of the camp. He did not see the works on the summit but did ride around the slopes, where he estimated there were 10,000 or 12,000 men, with ninety-two colours among them. He was much intrigued by the "fantastique habitt" of Buchanan's Highlanders, who numbered about 1,000 and carried swords, targes, some muskets, and bows and arrows. Aston considered that "the campe was not easy to be assaulted" and the Peace of Berwick meant that his view was never put to the test.

Defences in the industrial age

Only at **Eyemouth** did the Borders possess a port vulnerable to invasion from the sea, and two Victorian rifled guns can still be seen on Fort Point, which was reoccupied at times of danger in the 19th and 20th centuries.

At the time of greatest national peril, in 1940, none of the major strategic defence lines passed through the Borders, but a tactical response to the danger may best be seen at **Kelso**. The danger as perceived at the time came not only from the sea, but also from the air in the form of gliders and paratroops. Kelso was defended by a pillbox built to cover the approach to the town over Tweed Bridge and the street leading to the town square. Its presence is betrayed only by three loopholes in the stone parapet of the bridge approaches. Downstream from the bridge loopholes built in pairs into the riverside wall would have enabled riflemen to fire at anyone trying to cross the Tweed, although defenders would themselves have been vulnerable to fire from the higher ground on the Maxwellheugh side.

Such loopholes were inserted in existing walls to enable a small number of men to hold up an invading force, and other examples can be seen in the **Haining Gate** on The Green at Selkirk and in the parapet of **Ancrum Bridge**.

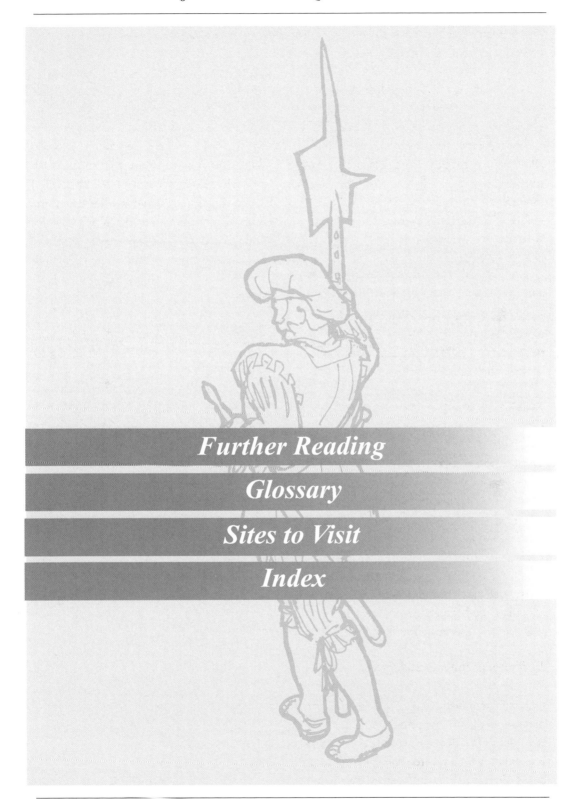

Further Reading

Dent, J & McDonald, R 1997. **Early Settlers in the Borders**. Scottish Borders Council, Newtown St Boswells.

Dent, J & McDonald, R 1998. **Christian Heritage in the Borders**. Scottish Borders Council, Newtown St Boswells.

Fraser, G M 1971. **The Steel Bonnets: the story of the Anglo-Scottish Border Reivers**. Pan.

Higham, N J 1993. **The Kingdom of Northumbria AD350 - 1100**. Alan Sutton, Stroud.

RCAHMCS 1915. **An Inventory of Monuments and Constructions in the County of Berwick**. HMSO, Edinburgh.

RCAHMS 1956. **An Inventory of the Ancient and Historic Monuments of Roxburghshire**. HMSO, Edinburgh.

RCAHMS 1957. **An Inventory of the Ancient and Historic Monuments of Selkirkshire**. HMSO, Edinburgh.

RCAHMS 1967. **Peeblesshire; An Inventory of the Ancient Monuments**. HMSO, Edinburgh.

Salter, M 1994. **The Castles of Lothian and the Borders**. Folly, Malvern.

Tabraham, C & Grove, D 1995. **Fortress Scotland and the Jacobites**. Batsford, London.

Tabraham, C 1997. **Scotland's Castles**. Batsford, London.

Yeoman, P 1995. **Medieval Scotland**. Batsford, London.

Glossary

Alba: kingdom of the Picts and Scots from c.844 to 1018.

Angli: a Germanic people who, during the decline of the Roman Empire, settled southern and eastern Britain, which became known as England (*Angle-land*).

baldrick: sword belt.

barmkin: walled courtyard attached to a tower house.

bastle: fortified farmhouse.

bastion: low, angular artillery tower with gun emplacements in the flanks.

Bernicia: Anglian kingdom approximating mainly to modern Northumberland.

bill: type of poleaxe.

Bonnie Prince Charlie: Charles Edward Stuart (the "Young Pretender"), claimant to the British throne and leader of the 1745 Rebellion.

breastwork: chest-high wooden protective screen, often used in conjunction with an earthen rampart.

bretasche: wooden projection from a wall-head to allow defenders to drop or shoot missiles down on attackers.

bridgehead: defended river crossing.

brigandine: a heavily reinforced protective jacket, also known as a jack.

buckler: small shield.

butts: practice targets for archers.

cap house: small watch-chamber at the top of a staircase, sometimes leading to a parapet walk.

cavalier: a gun emplacement raised to fire over the top of other guns.

chevaux de frise: literally "horses of Frisia" so-called because foot soldiers from Frisia (Germany) used a barrier of sharpened stakes as a defence against cavalry.

constable: keeper of a royal castle.

corbel: projecting stone block to support a beam or other feature.

crowstepped: a stepped gable.

Crusades: series of religious wars against non-Christians, which began in 1095 and continued intermittently thereafter.

culverin: 5″ (127mm) calibre muzzle-loading gun firing a 15lb shot.

curtain wall: high stone wall around a castle courtyard.

Dalriada: Irish kingdom which included parts of Argyll and the Western Isles in the Early Christian period.

donjon: main tower and final defence of a castle, also known as a keep.

demi-culverin: $4^{1}/_{2}$″ (114mm) calibre, muzzle-loading iron gun firing a 9lb shot.

enfilade: concentrate an otherwise scattered target from a crossfire position.

entresol: additional accommodation located between two main floors of a building.

escalade: an attack using ladders.

falcon: $2^3/_4''$ (70mm) calibre, muzzle-loading bronze gun firing 2lb shot and suitably mounted for use in a field campaign.

falconet: $2''$ (51mm) calibre muzzle-loading bronze gun firing 1lb shot and suitably mounted for use in a field campaign.

fief: land held as part of a feudal agreement.

fowler: $4^1/_2''$ (114mm) calibre breech-loading iron gun firing stone or grape shot and mounted on small wheels for use in fixed defences or in ships.

freestone: stone which can be worked in any direction, as opposed to greywacke or whin.

gabions: large baskets filled with earth or stones to form a temporary defence.

glacis: exposed slope on the outer side of a counterscarp bank.

Gododdin: a people known to the Romans as the Votadini, who were the subject of a British epic poem in which a band of warriors ride from Din Eiddyn to Catraeth.

grape shot: small cannon balls fired in a mass, usually at short range.

gun-loop: splayed opening in a wall for guns to fire through.

hackbutt: early firearm.

halberd: type of poleaxe.

harling: protective layer of cement applied to a wall.

jack: see brigandine.

keep: see donjon.

lock: firing mechanism on a firearm.

mangonel: huge catapult for hurling rocks and other missiles at a low trajectory.

militia: a part-time force established for local defence.

motte & bailey: earthwork castle consisting of an earth mound supporting a wooden tower with an adjacent courtyard surrounded by a ditch and palisade.

mural chambers: rooms built into the walls of a building.

New Model Army: force raised by the English Parliament in 1644-5.

Old Pretender: James Francis Stuart, claimant to the throne as son of James VII.

palisade: high wooden fence, used for defensive purposes.

parapet: wall or earth breastwork to protect troops.

pele: originally a palisaded enclosure, the term came to refer to any stone tower house.

poleaxe: long-handled axe equipped with a blade and a vicious point.

postern: secondary gate or doorway; normally a back entrance.

quoin: corner stone.

rake: position guns at a low level in a defence to provide maximum command over the approaches.

re-entrant angle: external corner where two wings of a building meet a right angles.

reiver: member of frontier society who engaged in kidnapping, rustling, extortion, burglary, and/ or murder as a way of life.

Roman de Fergus: 12th century romantic novel set mainly in the south of Scotland.

Rough Wooing: belligerent attempt to enforce a betrothal between young Queen Mary and Edward of England, in which the principal actions were Hertford's invasions of 1543-1547.

saker: $3^1/_8$" (79mm) calibre muzzle-loading bronze gun firing iron shot and suitably mounted for use in a field campaign.

sapping: undermining masonry to cause its collapse.

schiltron: traditional Scottish fighting formation of spearmen formed in a circle.

Scotti: an Irish people who conquered the natives of North Britain, and imposed their name upon the land.

Strathclyde: a British kingdom which occupied much of south-west Scotland during the Early Christian period.

string course: course of masonry projecting from the surface of a wall, often for a decorative effect.

surcoat: cloth garment worn over armour and sometimes charged with the wearer's coat of arms.

targe: see buckler.

trace: design for a fortification applied especially to angular artillery defences.

trebuchet: gigantic sling for hurling missiles at a high trajectory over castle walls, etc.

undermining: see sapping.

vassal: one bound by obligation to a feudal overlord.

weaponshaw: muster of a medieval armed host.

Wessex: kingdom broadly comprising the lands south of the Rivers Thames and Avon.

yett: a grid of iron bars used as a door.

zeppelin: military airship named after its German inventor.

Sites to Visit

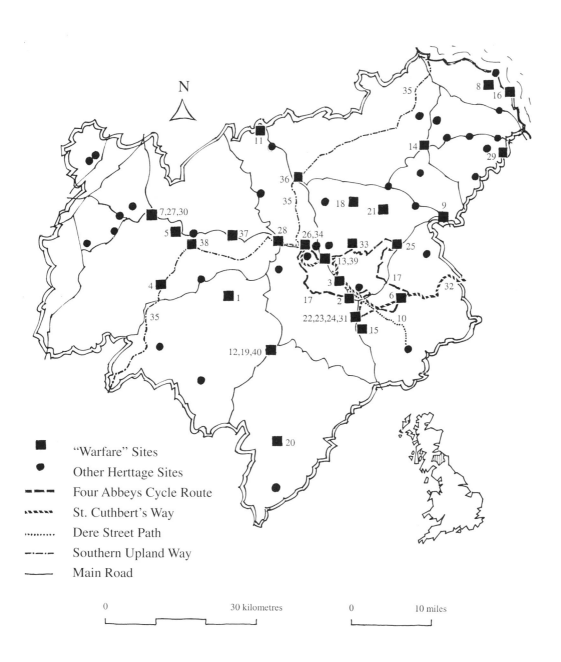

N

8
16
35
11
14
29
36
35
7,27,30
18
21
9
5
37
28
26,34
33
25
38
13,39
4
3
17
1
17
2
6
32
35
22,23,24,31
10
15
12,19,40
20

■ "Warfare" Sites
● Other Herttage Sites
- - - Four Abbeys Cycle Route
''''''' St. Cuthbert's Way
.... Dere Street Path
-·-·- Southern Upland Way
—— Main Road

0   30 kilometres   0   10 miles

Fig.34 *Sites to visit*

For details of opening times and admission charges please consult your nearest Tourist Information Centre, or contact:

Jedburgh Tourist Information Centre
Murray's Green
Jedburgh
Roxburghshire
TD8 6BE

1. Aikwood Tower, Selkirk; NT 420 260

Four storey tower house built around 1602 by Robert Scott. Recently renovated and restored with the adjacent byre, which now forms an interpretation centre for the poet, James Hogg.

There is no access to the castle and it should be viewed only from the road.

2. Ancrum Bridge; NT 638 237

Site of a skirmish in May 1549 involving the English under the Earl of Rutland and the French General D'Essé who had been charged with defending Jedburgh, but who had been forced to retreat northwards. Built into the bridge are a series of gun-loops dating from the Second World War.

3. Ancrum Moor; NT 618 271

On 27 February 1545 this was the scene of a battle between the Scots under the Earl of Angus and the English under Sir Ralph Eure and Sir Brian Layton. The battlefield can best be appreciated from Dere Street (see below).

4. Blackhouse Tower, Yarrow; NT 2807 2726

Late 16th century tower built by the Stewarts of Traquair. Visible (but not accessible) from the Southern Upland Way.

5. Cardrona Forest Walk, Traquair; NT 292 384

Cardrona Forest is situated on the south side of the River Tweed approximately three miles east of Peebles. There are parking and picnic facilities and three waymarked walks, two of which afford opportunities to view the remains of an Iron Age fort and the fortified medieval tower house "Cardrona Castle".

There is no access to the castle and it should be viewed only from the footpath.

6. Cessford Castle, Eckford; NT 738 238

Massive L-shaped tower overlooking the Kale Water. Built by the Kers of Cessford in the 14th century, it was originally surrounded by a stone and earth rampart now no more than 1.5m (5ft) high, and formerly bounded by a ditch.

There is no access to the castle and it should be viewed only from the road.

7. ***Chambers Institute, High Street, Peebles; NT 253 403***

This local history museum regularly holds exhibitions about the history and culture of the Borders.

8. ***Coldingham Priory; NT 903 659***

The church of St. Mary at Coldingham was founded in 1098. The remains of the south transept, cloister, chapter house and refectory, known as "Edgar's Walls" lie to the south of the present church. The medieval church blew up in 1650 after being bombarded by Oliver Cromwell's cannon.

9. ***Coldstream Museum, Market Place, Coldstream; NT 843 397***

A local history museum with an exhibition of material belonging to the Coldstream Guards.

10. ***Dere Street, Towford to St Boswells; NT 761 133 to NT 603 290***

Originally the strategic Roman road linking the legionary fortresses of York and Inchtuthil (Perthshire). This road became an important access into Scotland, which was used by later armies such as the Gododdin. The road crosses the battlefield of Ancrum Moor (see above).

11. ***Dere Street, Fala and Soutra; NT 402 580***

A short length of the Roman road (see previous entry) survives as earthworks where it approaches the escarpment at Soutra.

In the care of Historic Scotland

12. ***Drumlanrig's Tower, Hawick; NT 502 144***

16th century tower involved in the religious conflicts of King Charles II's reign, and later extended to form the town house of the Dukes of Buccleuch. Recently restored, it contains an exhibition on Border Reivers and a Tourist Information Centre.

13. ***Dryburgh Abbey, Mertoun; NT 591 316***

Premonstratensian Abbey founded around 1150 by Hugh de Morville. The best preserved buildings are in the east cloister range, and include a 16th century Commendator's House inserted into the canon's dormitory. The abbey was devastated on various occasions by English forces including 1322, 1385, 1544 and 1545.

In the care of Historic Scotland.

14. Duns Law, Duns;
  NT 785 547

A path leads north from Castle Street to the hill known as Duns Law, on which can be seen an Iron Age hillfort. The occupation of the hill by General Leslie's army during the First Bishops' War of 1639, has left a square redoubt, three small circular banks resembling gun emplacements, and the Covenanters' Stone. On the southern slopes of Duns Law are a series of well-preserved cultivation terraces which probably date to the medieval period.

15. Ferniehirst Castle, Jedburgh;
  NT 652 179

The seat of one of two main branches of the Kerr family, and scene of actions in various wars, particularly when it was captured from the English by the French garrison of Jedburgh in 1549. Spiral staircases in the castle turn to allow the left-handed Kerrs to defend the upper floors from attackers. The lowest storey dates from the 16th century. Restricted summer opening times.

16. Fort Point, Eyemouth;
  NT 941 649

A natural headland provided the site of successive English and French artillery forts in the 16th century. The ramparts still survive and provide some spectacular views of the rugged volcanic cliffs which now provide nesting places for many sea birds. The cliff path leads northwards to Coldingham and St. Abbs Head.

17. Four Abbeys Cycle Route;

A 88km (55 mile) circular cycle route linking the abbeys of Melrose, Dryburgh, Kelso and Jedburgh. This route explores the picturesque valleys of the Tweed, Teviot and Ale Water, and passes close to the sites of Smailholm Tower, Cessford Castle and Ancrum Bridge. Further details are available from Tourist Information Centres.

18. Greenknowe Tower, Gordon;
  NT 639 428

Built in the late 16th century by James Seton of Touch. The building is a classic L-shaped tower house consisting of a main rectangular block with a shorter wing.

In the care of Historic Scotland.

19. Hawick Motte;
  NT 499 140

Known locally as "Hawick Mote", this is a truncated grass-covered cone, of artificial construction, which was originally encircled by a defensive ditch and supported a timber tower. The motte probably dates from the 12th century when the Anglo-Norman family of the Lovels were granted land here by King David I.

20. Hermitage Castle, Castleton;
  NY 496 960

14th century castle with later additions and regarded as the most impressive of the medieval castles of the Borders. The castle is protected by defensive earthworks, including a 16th century gun-mount on the west side.

In the care of Historic Scotland.

21.   Hume Castle;
NT 704 413

Ancient seat of the Hume family, founded by William, son of the Earl of Dunbar in the 13th century. The base of the curtain wall, the castle well and a fragment of a central tower still survive beneath or within walls built in the late 18th century by the Earl of Marchmont.

22.   Castle Jail & Museum,
Castlegate, Jedburgh;
NT 647 201

The Victorian prison contains various exhibits relating to the history of Jedburgh, including finds made during excavations at the Dunion Iron Age hillfort.

23.   Jedburgh Abbey;
NT 650 204

Abbey of Augustinian canons founded by King David I. King Edward I of England stayed here and his soldiers took the roofing lead for siege engines. The abbey with the town bore the brunt of attacks in 1409, 1410, 1416, 1464, 1523, 1544, 1545 and was fortified in 1548 by the French.

In the care of Historic Scotland.

24.   Greyfriars Garden, Jedburgh;
NT 650 208

The foundations of a 16th century Franciscan friary, destroyed by the English in 1545, are displayed and interpreted in a picturesque garden which contains many medicinal herbs and local varieties of fruit tree.

25.   Kelso Abbey;
NT 728 338

Abbey of Tironensian monks who moved here from Selkirk around 1128. Abandoned for a time during the Wars of Independence, the abbey was severely damaged in 1522, 1542 and systematically dismantled in 1545 after its capture by Spanish mercenaries.

In the care of Historic Scotland.

26.   Melrose Abbey;
NT 548 341

Cistercian Abbey founded in or about 1136. Although this was one of Scotland's wealthiest monasteries, it suffered badly in wars, particularly in 1322, 1385, 1544 and 1545. The magnificent rebuilding of the late 14th and 15th centuries followed destruction by the English in 1385. The Commendator's House is now a museum and the Chapter House contains the burial of a heart, thought to be that of King Robert I.

In the care of Historic Scotland.

27.   Neidpath Castle, Peebles;
NT 236 404

Massive four storey L-plan tower house with courtyard range and gardens built in the late 14th century by William Hay of Locherworth. The castle is situated on a steep rocky crag overlooking the Tweed and is open to the public in the summer season.

28.   *Old Gala House, Galashiels;*
        NT 491 358

Originally a tower house built by the Pringles of Gala in the late 16th century. This building has been modified and extended on several occasions and now serves as the local museum and art gallery.

29.   *Paxton House, Hutton;*
        NT 931 519

The present mansion stands on the site of a fortified bridgehead constructed during the First Bishops' War of 1639. Pleasant walks beside the Tweed provide views across the river to the English bank where King Charles I's large military encampment once stood.

30.   *Peebles Town Wall;*
        NT 252 406

In 1570 the Burgh Council of Peebles commissioned the construction of a wall around the town. The only surviving section consists of a corner tower with gun-loops and two lengths of the adjoining wall.

31.   *Mary, Queen of Scots House,*
        Jedburgh; NT 651 206

16th century bastle house which has been preserved as a museum. It is thought to have been built by the Kerr family sometime after 1523 and is named Mary, Queen of Scots House due to local tradition that she spent time there in 1566.

32.   *St Cuthbert's Way,*
        Melrose to Lindisfarne;

A 100km (62.5 mile) cross border long distance walk linking Melrose Abbey and Lindisfarne. Part of the walk follows Dere Street, crosses the battlefield of Ancrum Moor and passes Cessford Castle. Further details are available from Tourist Information Centres.

33.   *Smailholm Tower;*
        NT 638 346

Early 16th century rectangular tower built on top of a rocky outcrop. This tower commands a fine panorama of the Cheviots, Lammermuirs, Eildons and the Merse. The tower was surrounded by a barmkin which enclosed a domestic range including a kitchen.

In the care of Historic Scotland.

34.   *Skirmish Field, Melrose;*
        NT 533 348

Scene of a battle on or around 25 July 1526 when Sir Walter Scott of Branxholm was unsuccessful in a bid to rescue the young King James V from the Earl of Angus. The site lies beside the River Tweed and is crossed by the Southern Upland Way footpath.

35. **Southern Upland Way;**

A 340 kilometre (212 mile) long distance coast to coast footpath from Portpatrick on the west to Cockburnspath on the east. The path passes Blackhouse Tower (**4**), Traquair House (**38**), Old Gala House (**28**), Skirmish Field (**34**), Melrose Abbey (**26**) and Thirlestane Castle (**36**). It also crosses the Tweed near Caddonlee, where the Scottish army traditionally assembled. Further details available from Tourist Information Centres.

36. **Thirlestane Castle, Lauder;**
       NT 533 479

Late 16th century castle built under the direction of John Maitland, Chancellor of Scotland. The building has been considerably enlarged and adapted since. The castle sits on the site of an earlier fortification occupied by King Edward II in 1324 and an artillery fort built by Protector Somerset in 1548. Very little survives of these earlier strongholds.

37. **Thornylee Viewpoint,**
       Innerleithen; NT 403 365

Car park and picnic site with sculpture and interpretative panels relating to the story of Elibank Castle and "Muckle Mou'd Meg" Murray. The picnic site offers fine views of the castle and the Tweed Valley.

38. **Traquair House;**
       NT 330 354

15th century tower house extended into a comfortable 16th and 17th century mansion which retains much of its historic character. The Earls of Traquair were strong supporters of the Stuart kings and the house played a part in the stories of the Marquis of Montrose and Bonnie Prince Charlie.

39. **Wallace Statue, Mertoun;**
       NT 591 326

Huge Old Red Sandstone statue erected in 1814 in honour of the Scottish patriot William Wallace, who was active in the Borders during the Wars of Independence.

40. **Wilton Lodge Museum, Hawick;**
       NT 493 145

Located within the attractive Wilton Lodge Park, the museum holds archaeological and zoological collections, with particular reference to Hawick district and Teviotdale.

Kings & Queens
From the Norman period to the Act of Union in 1707

Scotland

House of Canmore	
Malcolm III	1058-93
Donald III	1093-97
Duncan II	1094
Edgar	1097-1107
Alexander I	1107-24
David I	1124-53
Malcolm IV	1153-65
William I "the Lion"	1165-1214
Alexander II	1214-49
Alexander III	1249-86
Margaret	1286-90
Interregnum 1290-92	
House of Balliol	
John	1292-1313
Edward	1313-54
House of Bruce	
Robert I	1306-29
David II	1329-71
House of Stewart (Stuart)	
Robert II	1371-90
Robert III	1390-1406
James I	1406-37
James II	1437-60
James III	1460-88
James IV	1488-1513
James V	1513-42
Mary	1542-67
James VI	1567-1625

England

House of Normandy	
William I "the Conqueror"	1066-87
William II	1087-1100
Henry I	1100-35
Matilda	1135-54
House of Blois	
Stephen of Blois	1135-54
House of Plantagenet	
Henry II	1154-89
Richard I	1189-99
John	1199-1216
Henry III	1216-72
Edward I	1272-1307
Edward II	1307-27
Edward III	1327-77
Richard II	1377-99
Henry IV	1399-1413
Henry V	1413-22
Henry VI	1422-71
Edward IV	1461-83
Edward V	1483
Richard III	1483-85
House of Tudor	
Henry VII	1483-1509
Henry VIII	1509-47
Edward VI	1547-53
Mary I	1553-58
Elizabeth I	1558-1603

Union of the Crowns from 1603

James VI (I of England)	1603-25
Charles I	1625-49
Commonwealth	
Oliver Cromwell, Lord Protector	1653-58
Richard Cromwell, Lord Protector	1658-59
Restoration of House of Stuart	
Charles II	1660-85
James VII (II of England)	1685-88
House of Orange	
William III and Mary II	1688-1702
Anne	1702-14

Fig.35 Civil war and English intervention produced rival kings in Scotland in 1094 and between 1306 and 1354. England had rival monarchs from 1135-54 and from 1461 to 1471.

Index